MOTORCYCLING

AN ILLUSTRATED SOCIAL HISTORY

MOTORCYCLING

AN ILLUSTRATED SOCIAL HISTORY

ROGER FOGG

HALSGROVE

First published in Great Britain in 2013

British Library Cataloguing-in-Publication Data
A CIP record for this title is available from the British Library

ISBN 978 0 85704 197 5

HALSGROVE
Halsgrove House, Ryelands Business Park,
Bagley Road, Wellington, Somerset TA21 9PZ
Tel: 01823 653777   Fax: 01823 216796
email: sales@halsgrove.com

Part of the Halsgrove group of companies
Information on all Halsgrove titles is available at: www.halsgrove.com

Printed in China by Everbest Printing Co Ltd

CONTENTS

ACKNOWLEDGEMENTS

A large number of the photographs in this book have originated from the acclaimed Halsgrove Community History Series. In isolation they work well, but gathered together they become something more than simply a collection of old bike pictures. They can be seen as part of the wider world of motorcycling which in turn provides an extra context of time and place in which to view these machines. So all those who have provided images and memories for Halsgrove, and who have in turn contributed to this book, I say thank you once more for bringing alive those past times. More about the Community History Series can be found at www.halsgrove.com. Simon Butler, of Halsgrove, encouraged me to write this book, and directed me to sources and resources; I am extremely grateful to him for his encouragement and advice.

Many others have knowingly, and in some instances unknowingly, provided photographs and stories for this book. In a few cases, and hopefully within the context of the time and place, some poetic licence has been used for the captions. If these have been inaccurate, I apologise; however the autojumbles, on line auctions, and deceased estates from where many of the pictures originated cannot tell the stories themselves! I would like to thank the following people for the use of photographs and stories from their own collections: Jonathan Vickers, George Gunningham, Tom Seward, Morcom Moyle, Andrew Milton, John Lloyd-Hughes, Doc Kitts, Sam Edyvean, James Wolf, Colin Vincent, Julia Jennings, Reg Eyre, Sam Lovegrove, Peter Thomson from New Zealand, Sally Madgwick, Fran Parker, Barry Johnson, Martin Curl and Andrew Northam. The majority of the rest of the pictures came from the estate of the late Steve Stephens, and from the author's own collection.

INTRODUCTION

The motorcycle, since it became a recognisably distinct and unique form of transportation, has led a life which parallels in terms of technical advance, social convenience and delight that of the motor car, the aeroplane and the train. In the 120 years of their existence they have provided basic travel, often for the very first time; they have been used in war and peace, for racing and touring, for legal and illegal activities, for work and for play.

At its most basic, the bicycle with an engine, leaving but a single track in its path, has provided the world with an alternative means of mass movement, fashion statements, inspiration and individuality. Despite providing as many potential problems as solutions to everyday life, motorcycling still manages to maintain huge numbers of enthusiastic followers.

In the beginning there were few who believed that the internal combustion engine had a future. Most citizens of this country scoffed at the pioneers' attempts at locomotion without the use of horse or steam power. Very quickly attitudes began to change when manufacturers refined their products from spindly, unreliable and impractical machines into vehicles which were well thought out, strongly made and easily ridden by most ordinary people. The need for light pedal assistance on the steeper hills meant that pedals were still an essential part of the design, but factories which produced all the necessary ancillaries for the motorcycle; the magneto, the gearbox, the fuels and lubricants, the lights, chains, spark plugs and so on all contributed to its development.

The availability of fuels at rudimentary 'garages' and 'petrol stations', allied to selling, distribution and servicing facilities became commonplace. Those who had worked as blacksmiths, wheelwrights, wagon makers, watch and clock repairers, bicycle makers and so on, found that they could turn their hand to the new skills involved in vehicles which used the petrol engine. Horse traders too found a new vocation, instead of dealing in live animals they found novel ways of using their skills when buying and selling cars, motorcycles and indeed anything vaguely connected to the motor industry.

In the recording of its history, many authors tend to focus on the more spectacular events in which the motorcycle has played such an important role. An enquiring reader may wish to follow the racing successes of a particular marque, for instance, and how the factory designed and developed their machines over a period of years. Someone else, in the middle of a restoration might need to know when, and in what year, a certain part was fitted. There are a myriad of books available which allow the reader to help with the repair of their bike, how to make it go faster, and how to select a new machine. People have written adventure stories, about their real life journeys, biographies and even novels based around motorcycles. There are innumerable magazines and other publications devoted to the subject which seek to shed light on the exotic and unattainable and to see what the latest trends are. The world of motorcycling would be a poorer place if these were not available

However, this book focuses on the everyday experiences of ordinary riders who have recorded their personal, sometimes intimate, interaction with motorcycles through the use of their own photographs. In the early years, cameras were not common, and the images tend to be formal, set up by the cameraman who often required the subjects to keep absolutely still during the exposure of the film. As camera technology advanced, moving subjects could be captured, and film and cameras moved away from the professionals and into the hands of amateurs. As a result there exists in many homes an archive of photographs, snaps, postcards, bits and pieces; often locked away in drawers, kept in albums or boxes, out of sight yet still valued as part of the family history. And they all have stories attached, tales of who, why, what, where and when of the pictures.

In this new book, many of these photographs have been gathered together to provide an insight into the world of motorcycles as experienced by the hundreds of thousands of people who used them in a daily context as part of their ordinary life. The time period covered is mainly that in which British motorcycles were predominant; from the turn of the nineteenth century to the mid sixties. This book is almost exclusively about British bikes in a British context. It recognises that other brands were available, that other countries also manufactured motorcycles, and that most British manufacturers eventually succumbed to the onslaught of foreign made products. It acknowledges these things but concentrates on the Golden Era, when British was best, and everyone knew it.

The book is presented chronologically for convenience sake, although there appears to be recurring themes throughout the years, for instance some people seem obsessed with how many people they can cram on to a single machine, whilst animals, mostly dogs, appear frequently. Children are posed on saddles and prized motorcycles are proudly exhibited with the whole family strewn around. Holidays, picnics, weddings, outings all provide happy memories and are lovingly recorded and preserved in black and white images. This book reflects not just the history of the motorcycle, but also its place in the social development of this country.

Many of the manufacturers who went on to make the first motorcycles had their origins in the bicycle trade. Here a group of boys and their masters from Sidcot School, near Winchcombe in Gloucestershire, are on a cycle outing on their very early machines around the year 1885. The cycles represented here: Rover, Humber, Rudge, BSA, Sparkbrook and Bayliss Thomas are just some of the factories which gained much expertise in bicycle manufacturing before they launched motorised versions of their products at the end of the Victorian period. The bicycle still had some way to develop, the 'penny farthing' with its big wheels was still being made, the 'safety bicycle' with its smaller same-sized wheels and diamond frame was a few years away yet. The 'motor-cycle' had to wait until the small wheel bicycle was functioning reasonably effectively, imagine trying to put an engine into a 'penny farthing', although there are drawings of some who, unsuccessfully, tried!   PHOTO HALSGROVE CHS

This very early photograph shows S. J. Taylor of North Tawton, Devon, on his 1903 Excelsior. The primitive motorcycle of the time is well illustrated here. To start it you have to put it on its rear stand, which in turn has to be substantial enough to hold the weight of a pedalling rider, yet be capable of being folded back and used as a rear carrier when it was time to move off. There is no springing on this bike, except for the uprated bicycle saddle, so riding the unpaved Devon lanes of the time required much stamina and fitness on the part of the rider. Fuel was a problem; there were few places that sold it, and most people with petrol-engined vehicles had to order a store of it from a chemist. Tools for the frequent breakdowns were carried in the small saddlebag which as supplied by the manufacturers consisted of a couple of pressed out multi-purpose spanners and a bent wire screwdriver. It was a hard life being a motorcyclist at that time.   PHOTO HALSGROVE CHS

This is possibly the first motorcycle ever in Kettering, Northants, and it's quite an interesting machine. It looks very much like one of the very first Triumphs, made in 1903. There is no name on the tank, but Mauritz Schulte who was Triumph's chief engineer put a Belgian Minerva 2hp engine on to the sloping front down-tube of what was basically a reinforced bicycle frame and produced their first motorcycle. The machine shown here is also very similar to a Chater Lea; there are only minor differences, the strengthening bow in the front forks is added to a Chater Lea whilst Triumph retained an ordinary bicycle-style fork. The machine is balanced on its fold-under rear carrier, although close examination of the picture reveals an attempt, presumably by the cameraman, to scratch out any signs of the stand to make it seem that the rider is, in fact, moving. PHOTO HALSGROVE CHS

In the early part of the last century the motorised bicycle had become established pretty much as a solo machine. Difficulties arose when passengers needed to be carried, and several solutions were proposed. One, the forecar, involved removing the solo machine's front forks and wheel, and substituting instead an armchair suspended between two wheels on an axle Steering was difficult and heavy, the passenger was vulnerable and the motor struggled to shift a load far heavier than its design capability. Another version of this was the Tri-Car,

which, although it used the same principle, was designed from the start as a three-wheeler. It is not always easy to identify their makers; this photograph of a Northern Ireland registered machine is no exception, often only a few of a particular type were ever made. From what can be seen the engine is mounted above the steering head and there is some kind of gearbox arrangement which links it to the belt-driven rear wheel. The proud dad is not averse to seating his small daughter up front, albeit well wrapped up in blankets and an oilskin cover.

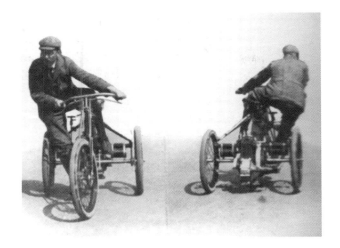

One of the most successful of the early motorcycles was the De Dion style of tricycle. The 1903 edition of *Motor Cycles and How to Manage Them* prints a letter from a correspondent asking why he had to lean when going round corners as he thought that the tricycle did not require any balancing when steering it. Thoughtfully they provided a couple of illustrations showing not only the reasons for leaning, but demonstrating clearly how it should be done, with photos taken from the front and the rear to back up their words. Many of the racing motorcyclists of the time actually came from the bicycle fraternity, their well developed calf muscles being extremely useful when light pedal assistance was called for.

This wonderfully evocative image is of an early attempt at passenger carrying by towing a trailer behind a motorcycle. Taken outside Edward Spencer's jewellers at 3 High Street, Wincanton in Somerset around 1905, the twin cylinder 3hp NSU motorcycle was one of the first motorcycles with the newly invented V-twin engine. Also fitted is NSU's own two-speed gear taken directly from the crank shaft and operated by the coffee grinder style handle on top of the tank. The Mills and Fulford trailer with its intricately woven wicker work and comfortable seating is attached to the bike beneath the seat. Although the bike was reasonably powerful, it still must have been hard work for the rider. The passenger sat in the dust, mud or spray kicked up by the bike's rear wheel. It was also not unknown for the graceful swan neck fitting which joined machine to trailer to break. The resultant tip up prompted the end of many a close relationship, and the use of trailers faded quite quickly as a fashionable means of passenger transport!
PHOTO HALSGROVE CHS

This wonderful photograph of Fred Batten's cycle shop in Cullompton, Devon, taken around the year 1904 shows a wealth of detail, and gives a wonderful insight into the business of early twentieth century transport. Mr Batten had obviously started off with bicycles, proudly boasting that he was the maker of the 'New Culme' cycle, but he was also an agent for BSA, Premier and Enfield if you chose one of their products over his. He listed on the board outside his shop that he sold tyres, pumps, free wheels, lamps, brakes, carriers, dress and mudguards, outfits and enamels. He also sold Bowden brakes and a variety of motor oils. The motorcycle, newly introduced as a means of transport to tempt his customers with in that year, is a Rex. Known as the King of Motor Bicycles, the Rex is a 3 hp model made in Coventry, and you could ride it away for just £52.10s. The dog contemplates what they have been doing to the car, which fits neatly into an opening to the rear of the building that was originally made for a horse and cart.   PHOTO HALSGROVE CHS

Above left: Zetland Street is in Southport, Lancashire, and this photograph was taken around 1903. It shows Mr Hough's emporium from where he sold motorcycles and their variants. Excelsior motorcycles were made in Coventry by Bayliss Thomas & Co Ltd and were arguably the first British motorcycle that went into volume production. Their engines were made by De Dion, MMC or Minerva. It's easy to see how the centre machine was turned from a solo into a forecar by the substitution of a comfortable wicker basket and upholstered cushion for the passenger between the two added-on wheels. All three of these models would have an exhaust valve actuated by an internal cam, whilst the inlet valve would have been automatic with a very weak spring and operated by the downward suction of the piston. They had surface carburettors and a battery that needed to be kept fully charged. It was bad enough trying to pedal off a solo, but it must have been particularly hard trying to get the forecar going when fully laden

Above right: Frank Hough's in Zetland Street sold mostly bicycles. He had decided that this would be a lucrative business, the old 'ordinary' or 'penny farthing' had gone, and the 'safety' with its diamond frame was now all the rage. Still, he couldn't afford to ignore the new-fangled petrol engine, and he branched out into cars and motor bikes as well. Frank Hough in his later years created his own brand, specialising in invalid carriages, tricycles and other bespoke pedal cycles. He stopped trading in the late fifties, and eventually retired to Cornwall. This picture, developed from a glass plate, shows the interior of his Edwardian shop in Southport.

In 1903 Tom Silver on a 3 HP Quadrant motorcycle rode from John o' Groats to Land's End in a time of 64 hours and 29 minutes. Silver had to pedal much of the way, his willing little engine needing quite a lot of lpa (light pedal assistance). His plan was to get to a given place at a set time where willing assistants would attend to his machine, while he swallowed an egg sandwich and a stiff drink or two. Sympathetic racing cyclists and Quadrant customers assisted him across dubious road junctions and through busy towns, whilst organised food and supplies awaited him along the route. As can be seen in the photograph, the bike had no suspension at all, and the spidery frame and narrow saddle could not have made for the most comfortable ride. Tom failed to keep within many hours of his schedule, the delays caused through punctures, getting lost despite all precautions and mechanical failures, all contributed to the time lost. PHOTO J VICKERS

The 1904 Vibrationless 3¼hp Rex 'Air Draught' of 1904 was priced at 50 guineas according to the advertisement placed in *The Motor* on 19 January 1904. This brought the King of Motor Bicycles 12 months ahead of its imitators. Features included the Rex Air Draught cylinder, foot rim brake, improved patent silencer, exhaust valve lifter and an improved surface carburettor, all with twelve months guarantee. The Rex Motor Manufacturing Company Ltd of Coventry was apparently on the War Office List and claimed to have the largest combined output of tri cars, cars, and motor bicycles of any British manufacturing firm. The Air Draught cylinder involved extra finning around the valves with a plate attached which directed cool air to that area. This proud owner has fitted an early wickerwork sidecar although he could quite easily have bought and fitted a tri-car arrangement to the front of his machine and achieved the same passenger carrying abilities.

Below: Another Rex, this time a 3½hp V-twin from around 1905 with an atmospheric carburettor, but still reliant on coil rather than magneto for ignition. The photograph was taken in Cumberland and demonstrates the Rex's simple design made out of first class materials. The front fork, with its sprung axle, exactly predated the action and geometry of today's telescopic fork. To boost their sales Rex had generous part exchange scheme for their new models, although this threatened to land them in deep financial water. There are no lights fitted to this model, and the rear carrier can be folded down to use as a stand to aid pedal starting whilst the machine is stationary

ALFRED F. GIBBINGS, CARRIAGE BUILDER,
RELIANCE WORKS, CULLOMPTON.

In 1904 wagon and carriage makers were still going full tilt, producing a wide range of two- and four-wheeled horse drawn vehicles. There was a bewildering variety of design shapes and forms, some were made to suit local conditions, others were bespoke whilst yet again there was a market for 'off the shelf' vehicles. Here, Gibbings' Carriage works of Cullompton in Devon have two of their products on display outside their shop. However the future is looming in the shape of the bicycle, and even the motorcycle. The bike is a Quadrant, dated around 1903, and is very similar to the one that Tom Silver rode from 'End to End' in a record breaking time. 'The Quadrant' and 'The Excelsior' were said to have done more to demonstrate the practicability of the motorcycle than any other makes. Gibbings would also sell you an 'Alldays' motorcycle or car, and could provide Dunlop motor tyres for them as well. PHOTO HALSGROVE CHS

Below: Wardill's Cycle shop in Pound Street, Carshalton manufactured their own bicycles, but they were also agents for Minerva motorcycles. Minerva was a Belgian company which manufactured complete machines, and also sold 'loose' engines to the trade or to anyone else who wanted to install one in a frame of their own design. The three motorcycles in this 1905 picture are not too easy to identify, but probably the one on the left facing the camera is a P & M, a Yorkshire made bike with a sloping engine, the centre machine is a Bradbury whilst the third is a Minerva. Wardill sold petrol in cans, supplied by Shell and Pratt's, and they also stocked Warwick tyres. The Minerva has its front number plate attached to the headlight in order to provide illumination for its registration. The bicycle wheel and front forks on the pole probably served as a guide for the flag rope and, as with many other early garages, Wardill's also repaired phonographs and you could purchase records from them. PHOTO HALSGROVE CHS

The firm of NSU had been established in Germany back in Victorian times, and quickly latched on to the newly-invented internal combustion engine. They exported their machines all over the world, and this V-twin was photographed in Birmingham around 1904. It was quite an expensive purchase, and as an extra, has been fitted with NSU's two speed gear pulley on the crankshaft. The poor boy in the sailor suit is the epitome of starched correctness which was expected of middle class Edwardian children. On no account smile, move or speak. Probably the dog had the same instructions!

Below: This is a Clement Garrard 'Torpedo Model' motorcycle from 1904. They were made in Birmingham, the frame parts were supplied by Norton and the engines were small French-built Clements; they were only produced for a few years and not many have survived. The mystery with this one is that it has a larger De Dion or similar engine, with a magneto and carburettor. It was not difficult to fiddle around with different combinations of frame and engine, and many home brewed one-off specials were made by skilled mechanics in their back sheds. It is Surrey registered, perhaps the younger man fancied something with a bit more power, and got the older man, whose hand rests protectively on the handlebar, to make it for him.

At the beginning of the automotive industry there was no real distinction between cars and lorries, motorcycles and voiturettes. They all had the newly invented internal combustion engine to power them and as such appealed to the same kinds of people, no matter what they chose to drive or ride.

By 1905 however the various classes of vehicle had been demarcated into groups which are still accepted, even up to present times. Magazine proprietors were quick to exploit this potential market, and produced dozens of publications to inform and enlighten their readers on the subject. The examples shown here are representative of those early years, and nowadays provide fascinating insights into the infant world of motoring for modern historians.

Patents are a fascinating source of historical information, in many fields, not just that of motorcycling. There are many would-be inventors who wish to claim their share of immortality by patenting some breakthrough that they have masterminded, yet in truth most patents are on very small improvements in very small things. Screws and fittings are one example, yet if you get it right then you can make a fortune. A motorcycle manufacturer who patented a hand grenade with spark plug that was to be lowered by fishing line on to an enemy Zeppelin by a fearless pilot was summarily dismissed. Another, with only loose connections to the two-wheel trade patented, the little opening catch for tins of boot polish and collected royalties on each tin subsequently manufactured; it made him a millionaire.

Above: Coventry built Rex Motorcycles enjoyed a considerable vogue in the early 1900s. Their star rider was Harold Williamson who held the End To End record for them over a period of four years. The machines had up-to-the-minute designs including a very effective spring fork, a free engine clutch and a two-speed gear. This shot shows a Rex, possibly Williamsons own, and written on the tank are the words 'World record ride 56,500 miles to date and only a Rex can do it'. The exact location of The Black Bull is not known, however the other motorcycles are Minerva's with Edinburgh registration numbers.   PHOTO J VICKERS

Opposite, top: The Durham Ox was a castrated bull, born in 1798 near Darlington that became famous for its weight, size and shape. It was an early example of the Shorthorn breed of cattle and defined the standards by which all others were judged. The location of this particular pub is at Shrewley Common in Warwickshire and this group of riders was photographed around 1910, and although most of the bikes are difficult to identify, there are at least two Triumphs on view, identified by their unique forks. A day out for the local club; flat hats and rain coats are universally worn. The group of men in the background are all holding push bikes, and just possibly looking on enviously!

Opposite, bottom: Lined up outside the Atheneum in Barnstaple are members of the Barnstaple and District Motorcycle and Light Car Club. Light cars could join in with the club's motorcycling activities because of their common ancestry. Morgan, BSA and a whole host of other motorcycle manufacturers produced three-wheelers or cyclecars which owed much of their design and motive power to the world of two wheels. In this group are members of the club with a variety of motorcycles from the early twenties including Triumph, Douglas and BSAs whilst at the end of the row there is what looks like an early Lagonda. It was from these types of clubs that competitive events for ordinary clubmen were first organised on a local basis, but there were also social excursions, picnics, treasure hunts, paper chases and the like for families and the less combative members. The Atheneum, on The Square in Barnstaple, was founded in 1888 as a free library and museum for local people.   PHOTO HALSGROVE CHS

Dr Good of High Bickington in Devon with a brand new 1908 Triumph single speeder. Well used and covered in red Devon mud, the engine has been working hard and there are traces of some oil leaking around the crankcase. As a result of successes in the 1907 TT races where their machines came second and third, improvements in valves and piston rings were incorporated into the very latest production models made at Triumph's Priory Street factory in Coventry. In 1908, the year Doctor Good bought his bike, Triumphs actually won the TT in the Isle of Man. No doubt this influenced his thoughts and really he could not have bought a better bike at the time to do his rounds and attend to his patients. PHOTO HALSGROVE CHS

Below: In 1910 Dr Good had his surgery in what is now the Post Office in High Bickington. He obviously liked Triumph motorcycles; this one is from 1911 and has a two-speed rear hub, which gave him the luxury of not just a high and low gear but also a neutral. This meant that he did not always have to pedal like mad to get it going after a stop. The Triumph was such a good bike that it would get up most hills anyway, but arriving at a patients all hot and sweaty was not the best plan. The spaniel not wishing to be left out of the photograph is called Rex. The car is a 1912 single-cylinder 7hp Swift. The car makers Swift were tied up with the motorcycle makers of the same name, although the motorcycle was basically a badge engineered Ariel. PHOTO HALSGROVE CHS

Motorcycles, being the main means of transport, deserved their own garages. Here is 'The Motor House' of a middle class suburban family of 1912, with everyone relaxing in deck chairs on the lawn outside. There were many articles in the magazines of the time as to what might go into the perfect, what we might nowadays call, a shed. There were wooden trestles on which to mount the bikes, shelves and hooks for the tools, a corner to store the oils and petrol, another area where basic machine tools such as a lathe might be sited and a block and tackle for lifting engines as and when necessary. The Triumph and Gloria sidecar are from that year.

As long as there are people who drive or ride motorcycles, indeed any powered vehicles, there will always those who want to compete on them. One of the most popular of the record attempts at the time concerned the 880 mile journey from John o' Groats to Land's End. In June 1911, Ivan Hart Davies set off from John o' Groats with his eyes firmly set on gaining the record. Riding a new 3½hp Triumph, he left at 3am, and got to Carlisle in 12 hours, with but a single puncture, two belt fasteners broken and a lost horn. From then on things got harder, and after a night's hard riding found himself in Wigan for 6.00pm, then on to Tewkesbury as night began to fall once again, Moonlit

riding through Bridgewater and further on meant he made good time despite having two more punctures and a lengthened valve. He motored on to Bodmin, where he fell off on a corner. In Penzance more petrol was taken on, but the bike wouldn't start until it was pushed to the top of Market Jew Street. Four miles from Land's End he had another flat tyre, and he finished the last mile and a half riding on the rear rim. Hart Davies finished the last 100 yards at a gallop, and beat the record in an incredible time of 29 hours 12 minutes. The official time still stands today, having been declared the final record for fear of excessive and illegal speeding by others seeking to go even faster.

A motorcycle meeting in rural Denbighshire in 1912 brings out the very latest and finest two-wheeled machines available at the time. There is a Rudge Multi with its variable gearing, a V-twin Indian newly arrived from America, a German made NSU with its unique design of front forks, a Bradbury and a fifth unidentified machine. All had their own special selling points and all were very capable of coping with the steep hills and rutted roads of that part of Wales. The Bradbury, which was made in Oldham, had the crankcase brazed into the frame. It is interesting to contrast the various lights on these bikes, from none at all on the Indian, to a bicycle lamp on the NSU and a huge Lucas on the Bradbury.

Below: The police seemed to have acquired motorcycles as part of their official transport in the years immediately preceding the First World War. Some forces just bought in a few machines, kept them in the colours and livery of the manufacturer and simply issued them to those officers who could ride. It was not until 1914 that they were more formally used for traffic control and in situations where they might perform more efficiently than a car or a horse. This is a bit of a mystery photograph. The sergeant's machine probably predates the photo by a few years, although it's not easy to identify what make it is. On the wall above the doorway WCC 1910 is carved, whilst the registration number is one issued in Liverpool. The fact that he is not wearing a traditional style helmet may indicate that he was of a more senior rank than may at first appear.

The 1300 foot high Porlock Hill has always been a formidable climb with its one-in-four gradients and hairpin bends. The first car up was driven by the noted rally driver S F Edge, basically for a bet. The first motorcycle to successfully climb it was in 1909, whilst the first charabanc made it in 1916. In the early days it was used competitively, and this picture shows a car attempting the muddy curves. The two girl spectators immediately in front of the cyclecar, (possibly a GN), and watching it with great interest are Winifred and Grace Burgess, whose father owned the shop down the hill in the village. The onlookers beneath their umbrellas include at least one motorcyclist whose bike looks like a Scott. The picture was taken in 1912. The hill was included in many road trials of the period because of the testing nature of the climb, it often featured for example in the London to Land's End Trial. PHOTO HALSGROVE CHS

Below: This is a 3½hp Humber from around 1910 or 1911. It is fully equipped with lights, horn and pannier bags and built into the rear wheel is a ROC two-speed gear, although a more basic model with single speed and pedalling gear could also be obtained from the factory if you couldn't afford this more luxurious version. (ROC stood for 'Ride on Comfort', the author Sir Arthur Conan Doyle had a financial interest in this company). The tube projecting from the exhaust pipe is in fact a whistle, operated by the rider's foot, and there is a leather mud flap attached to the front mudguard to protect the engine from mud thrown up by the wheel. The sidecar is of Humber's own manufacture, there was a choice of cane, wicker, coach-built or commercial bodies available for purchasers to choose from. The unknown rider was no doubt influenced in his purchase by the Works' backed competition events, including the TT Races, which Humber enthusiastically supported at the time.

'BAT AT 'T AGAIN' says the slogan on the 1912 Bat motorcycles advert. Over a route through the wilds of Cumberland, up precipitous mountain tracks, around sharp turns and on roads with truly appalling surfaces, the BAT ridden by S T Tessier gained full honours and made a non-stop run. Made in London, at the factory in Penge, the BAT was named after the firm's founder, Mr Batson. The company had produced the first spring frame to appear on the British market and built on its reputation by proclaiming that BAT stood for Best After Test. The machine depicted here has an Armstrong hub and a V-twin JAP engine which was available in sizes of 650, 770, 964 and 980cc. Note the unique design of leading link front forks, forty years before the Earles type became much more widely used. In 1913 BAT finished 11th in the TT on a very similar machine to this one, ridden by W H Bashall.

Below: What happens with this 1910 Zenith Gradua is that the variable engine pulley, of which the top is changed through a coffee grinder style handle on the top tube, and a simultaneous correction of the belt length through sliding the rear wheel to and fro in the rear fork slots, gives an infinite number of gears within a bottom ratio of 5½ to 1, and the highest of 3 to 1. The gentleman is demonstrating how the remarkable climbing powers of the JAP engined Zenith worked, giving it an unfair advantage over lesser machines, and in fact being barred from single gear classes in hill climbs. Zenith successfully exploited this ban on their tank badge, which showed one of their products with the word BARRED scrawled across the name.

Charles Pratt died in 1891 but not before he had established an important business that replaced whale oil which was used for lighting with fossil-fuel oil produced from wells in the United States. The empire which he founded was still in its automotive infancy when this 1899 advert was published in *The Automotor and Horseless Vehicle Journal*. Barrels and tins of motor spirit were delivered by rail or horse and cart to stockists, and the contents were transferred into the customers' own containers. This dangerous practice only really ceased with the introduction of underground, sealed storage tanks and proprietory petrol pumps after the First World War.

1911 – 1919

The Garage of Mr Cecil C Hann in the Dorset village of Beaminster was an agency in 1912 for RCH cars. RCH stood for R C Hupp, who had invented the Hupmobile in America and then left the firm to make his own petrol-engined vehicles using his initials as the company's logo. They were not terribly well received, particularly in this country, and Mr Hupp soon after turned his attentions to electrically powered vehicles. Mr Hann on the other hand stuck with the internal combustion engine which was something he knew about. The big V-twin Sunbeam and the smaller

Douglas leaning against the wall in his garage are evidence of his involvement with two wheelers. The vehicle behind the RCH seems to be a crudely built special; the suspension and steering appear home made, and the body looks quite agricultural. The single, central carbide headlight and smaller electric lights would have provided some night time illumination, but in contrast to the RCH, the whole vehicle looks decidedly amateurish in its construction.

PHOTO HALSGROVE CHS

Mrs Clara Hawke and her mother Mrs White are seen together on this 1911 Triumph sidecar outfit at Helston. Originally this would have been a single-speed machine, the belt working directly from the engine crankshaft pulley. Starting would have been by pedalling hard and dropping the decompression lever. This would not have been easy with the sidecar attached, so NSU, the German firm, invented an ingenious two-speed epicyclic gear which replaced the Triumph front pulley and provided two gears and a neutral. The little tram handle device to the rear of the petrol tank winds a cam and lever arrangement which effectively alters the gearing ratios. Mrs Hawke is sitting side saddle; presumably the owner and driver of the outfit is taking the photograph. Other things worthy of note, beside the ladies hat firmly tied down with a scarf, is the carbide light perched precariously on the fork springs where Triumph thought they would most stable. Note also the filthy mud flap on the front mudguard. This was an expensive vehicle for its time, and had obviously been bought with the intention of being ridden properly rather than simply as a passing fancy.   Assuming the lady in the sidecar is about 70 years old, then she would have been born around the year 1840, the year when the first British Colonists reached New Zealand. PHOTO HALSGROVE CHS

Opposite, top: This joyous picture of three boys just mucking about in a sidecar outfit sums up all the pleasures and happiness of youthful enthusiasm and companionship. The bike is a Triumph from 1911, the boy in the sidecar is Herbie Duke and the place is Creech St Michael near Taunton, Somerset. Roy Batson in his book *A land Beyond the Ridge* summed up the time thus; 'I can still recall those first rides, the wild, swift rush through the winter lanes, the leafless trees and hedges ripping past on either hand, the roar of the big engine in my right ear and the air chilled like wine'. In a few short years the young boys on the motorcycle would be caught up in the dreadful events of August 1914, but for now at least their laughter and pleasure were unconfined.   PHOTO HALSGROVE CHS

Opposite, bottom: Parked outside Mr Child's cycle repair business in Hethersett, a village in Norfolk, is an Ariel attached to a beautifully made wickerwork sidecar. Ariels produced this new machine in 1910 using a 482cc White and Poppe engine, the distinctive feature of which was advertised as 'The Ariel with the valves a mile apart'. In fact the T-headed motors valves were 4½ inches from each other, which helped produce a claimed power output of 3½hp at 2000rpm. You could buy an Ariel like this in 1914 for between £47-10s and £60-15s, depending on whether you had a fixed gear belt drive, or as on the model shown here, a chain-cum-belt drive with the Ariel three-speed countershaft gearbox. The sidecar was another 15 guineas fitted at the factory. The Ariel factory started by manufacturing bicycles in the late 1890s, and sold them through the firm of Cycle Components Ltd. In this photograph Mr Childs has a brand new bicycle for sale, and possibly also is in the process of building one up from scratch, a practice common at the time.   PHOTO HALSGROVE CHS

The group of people gathered around the front of the Stamford Bridge Hotel are dressed for cold weather, the kind of conditions that are to be expected in an English winter. They are watched by a small gaggle of boys who look on enviously at the big Royal Enfield sidecar outfit all kitted out and ready to take on whatever nature can throw at it. The photograph would have been taken immediately prior to the First World War, and the London registered 771cc side-valve JAP engined Royal Enfield in full view was not cheap; 80 guineas with its sidecar attached. Interestingly the pillion seat is mounted sideways so that the passenger can rest both feet on the rear of the sidecar chassis. There are those who, tongue in cheek, suggest that the 'Bad Boy' motor cycling image had its origins in the reversed-hat-and-goggle wearers' style of dress, examples of which can be seen in this picture. In fact, it just stopped the hat being blown off at the staggeringly high speeds of over 30mph which these machines could achieve.

This portrait of a smiling young man was given away free to readers of *Motorcycling* in July 1913. Tim Wood was the winner of that year's Senior TT riding a Scott. His average speed for the 262½ miles was 48.9 mph, with a lap record of the 37½ mile circuit of 43 minutes 10 seconds. Contrast that with the lap times of John McGuinness a hundred years later, when he lapped in 17 minutes 12 seconds and averaged 131½mph on a Honda! One hundred years ago the clothes were also made of leather, but the head gear merely provided warmth rather than any degree of protection in a crash. All the tapes on Tim's body are to hold the numbered vest firmly on his back. PHOTO *MOTORCYCLING*

The Port of Falmouth has always played an important part in the maritime history of England. It was where the packet ships which took the mails to and from the colonies began their journey, news of the Nelson's victory at Trafalgar first reached these shores on the local quayside, and it was where clippers bringing in tea and cotton called in for their 'orders'. Belletti's Motor works, close to the docks, was able to benefit from the spending power of sailors, passengers, and all the other trades associated with the waterfront. They could hire out launches or hearses, they could put your vehicle over their inspection pit, and they would have a go at fixing your motorcycle. The older vehicles inside the garage were bought cheaply and used to transport passengers and their luggage between station and hotels, hence the name 'station wagons'. And if you wanted a cup of tea while you waited then Jenkin's tea rooms next door was the perfect place for refreshments.

This picture of a couple from Yorkshire out in their Scott and sidecar was taken just before the First World War. There are a lot of accessories on this machine, the speedometer, the electric horn and expensive lights with large generator

attached to the sidecar, not to mention the fold down windscreen and coverings for the passenger's comfort. The Scott, with its kick start mechanism was an ideal sidecar machine and would later be developed by the factory into a machine gun carrier using a triangulated frame on which to mount the weapons. A A Scott also suggested that, solo, his motorcycle was quite capable of carrying a machine gun whose magazine would fit neatly into the open frame. Meanwhile this couple have wrapped up against the cold and wet of the North Yorkshire autumn.

The White Horse Pub, which was once part of the village of Maiden Newton, was an old coaching inn on the road from Crewkerne to Dorchester in Dorset. It was the inspiration in part for the setting for Thomas Hardy's story *Tess of the D'Urbervilles*. This scene, from about 1910, of that small rural community would barely have changed since Hardy visited. The only motorised vehicle is the solo motorcycle; the horse-drawn bread van has just made a delivery, the women in Edwardian costume are gossiping and the dogs are lazily doing not much. The road would have been a dust covered track meandering across the high chalk ground between summer scented hedges, a great contrast to the busy A356 which it has now become.

Many of the old coaching houses and pubs were lifesavers for motorcyclists caught in sudden downpours or having unexpected breakdowns. The Hoops, not far from Clovelly, and on the main road between Bude and Barnstaple was one such place. Here a 1913 Scott sidecar pauses in bright sunshine for a welcome glass of beer. In the early years this 13th century inn was supposedly a haunt of smugglers and other such villains, as well as seafarers of the likes of Grenville, Drake and Raleigh. More recently it has become a highly regarded pub and restaurant. Scotts were particularly suited to the hilly North Devon countryside, as they were to their native Yorkshire. Alfred Angas Scott, their designer used all chain drive, two speeds, a clutch and most interestingly a kick start, which he is credited with inventing.

From 1907 to 1914 the firm of Alldays and Onions produced cars, motorcycles and other industrial equipment from their factory in Sparkbrook, Birmingham. This is an Alldays 'Matchless', a name which had nothing to do with the Matchless Company owned by the Colliers. It dates from just before the First World War and has a 350cc side-valve engine of their own manufacture; it had sprung aluminium footboards for extra comfort, used 'Brampton Bi Flex' forks, and was started by using a hand crank on the rear wheel. The sheep in this snowy Denbighshire scene seem unimpressed by the old motorcycle; perhaps if it were bringing them some feed they might be more enthusiastic.

Below: From the beginnings of two-wheeled sport there has always been a market for stunt riding. First it was done by intrepid bicycle riders, doing loops and jumps on their push bikes, but although it paid well, casualty rates were high. In 1915 The Tom Davies Trio, all equipped with specially adapted Levis Popular two-stroke motorcycles of 211cc began to try their luck on the 'Silodromes', built for cyclists. One such attraction involved circulating in a kind of monster fruit-bowl-shaped mesh cage, which rose up from the ground whilst attached to strengthened poles. Later, and as speeds increased, this was adapted to a more rigid construction of wood which formed a large circular shape, spectators being able to stand at the top and look down at the daredevils inside. Quite soon this became known as the 'Wall of Death', and was to become a familiar sight and sound at fairgrounds all over the country.

THE WORLD'S FAMOUS TOM DAVIES TRIO ON THEIR LEVIS

It was often the case that proud owners gave their bikes names. This particular 8hp Zenith was called 'Oliver'. Lawrence of Arabia had names for all his Broughs – 'Boanerges' was the first followed by a series of 'Georges'. There have been some really creative names: 'Rumbleguts', 'Gunga Din', 'Two Tails', 'Parasite' and the heartfelt 'Money Pit'. This Zenith, pictured in West Cornwall around the early twenties, shows that some minor roads had still not received a coating of tar; the ruts and puddles created by horse drawn traffic, cattle and other vehicular traffic could still catch out the unwary rider. Better button up your flying helmet and hope for the best!

Below: This group of off-duty naval officers form a shooting party at an unknown country estate in the south of England. Drinks having been served by younger ratings, the men are about to embark on their motorcycles to a remote corner of the property where they can blast away at the pheasants and partridges to their hearts' content. From left to right the machines are a 1914 Henderson Four, 1914 Royal Enfield 400cc V-twin, a Belgian Sarolea and a 1914 Royal Enfield 2¾hp model. A few months after this shot was taken, all the men would have been placed on a war footing, and possibly had to face the German fleet at Jutland.

On His Majesties Service, both rider and 4¼hp Model K BSA have been called up to fight in Kitchener's army. There was always a policy of impressing civilian property into the services if the situation warranted it. Here it seems that the Kent registered motorcycle has had its front mudguard hurriedly painted with OHMS, yet it still wears its civvy street registration number and there is no attempt at camouflage paint. The bike is well equipped with lights and there is even a carrier for a spare belt attached to the rear carrier. The rider has very clean boots, although the bike seems to have rather more mud around its edges than might have passed a sergeant's inspection. PHOTO J VICKERS

The rider sitting astride this Model 'D' Triumph looks as if he would be rather more at home on a horse than on a motorcycle. Horses of course played a hugely important role in the First World War, but in a conflict which rapidly developed into a highly technical and mechanical war of attrition, they had their limitations. Many of the old cavalry regiments were issued with fighting vehicles; armoured cars, lorries, motorcycles, tractors and of course the first of the tanks to become operational. So, despite some reservations, this gentleman seems happy enough with his lot, and at least he doesn't have to find hay and water for his mount. PHOTO J VICKERS

Above left: There are a variety of motorcycles visible in this posed photograph of the Mobile Motorcycle Machine Gun Section 'receiving a sudden call' somewhere on the Western Front. There are solo Triumphs, Douglases and even a Sunbeam, but the combinations are worthy of an extra look. The firms of Clyno, Enfield, Matchless, P & M, New Imperial, Royal Ruby and Scott were amongst those who supplied sidecar outfits for the war effort. The Clyno outfits which are featured in this picture clearly have the spare wheel attached to the rear of the motorcycle, whilst their long wheelbase gave them great stability. Machine guns were Vickers Maxim, with the gunner firing either forwards or backwards. Ammunition boxes could be carried on board, and some were even capable of carrying stretchers. PHOTO HALSGROVE CHS

Above right: There may have been a few remarks in German about the quality of British motorcycles, but even if you have to change the rear spark plug on your Douglas, there is no avoiding the fact that you are there to guard a column of prisoners of war. In 1914 captured soldiers were sent to a permanent camp in Dorchester, and soon other temporary, permanent and makeshift prisons were established all over the country. 1917 saw extensive use of POWs in road building, quarrying and land reclamation; this was allowed under the Geneva Convention. Only four prisoners ever managed to escape, two made it home, whilst the other two drowned in the North Sea. Most were content with their lot and gave little trouble to the guards, members of the Royal Defence Corps. PHOTO HALSGROVE CHS

Below: At the start of the Great War the Government was looking at ways of replacing the horse with powered two wheelers for carrying messages. Motorcycles up to that point were still quite primitive, but the Triumph factory responded by making their new 'Model H' specifically for the task. Triumphs had already gained a great reputation for ruggedness and reliability, but their new model finally did away with bicycle-style pedals and rear hub gears. Although still belt driven, the Model H had both a gearbox and a clutch. Here, works rider and tester Dan Young, together with his companion, stops for a rest whilst out testing new bikes. The DU registration from Coventry suggests that the bikes are out on factory trade plates. Triumph went on to make 30 000 of this model by the end of the war; they were so reliable that they were nicknamed 'Trusty', (although in fact the factory first used that word in their publicity half a dozen years before). PHOTO J VICKERS

In the muck and the mud of the Great War trenches, communications were vital. Motorcycles proved very useful for carrying messages, but here we can see that they were not the only means of getting reports and signals back to HQ. Pigeons had been used as message carriers for hundreds of years, but during the First World War, before the advent of proper wireless telegraphy, they came into their own. Over 100 000 birds were used altogether, with 95 per cent of them getting through and delivering messages which were placed inside a tiny canister attached to one of their legs. One of the most famous pigeons was called Cher Ami, which flew 25 miles in 25 minutes with a message back to HQ, thus enabling a group of 200 American soldiers to be rescued from shelling by their own side. Cher Ami was in fact shot by the Germans as he flew overhead, but managed to complete his mission despite his injuries. In this 1917 photograph a British soldier carries a pigeon basket on his back as he sets off for the front line on his Douglas. The mobile pigeon loft mounted on the truck followed the troops as necessary. PHOTO HALSGROVE CHS

Corporal Bromley Penny was no ordinary Despatch Rider in the Great War. Although used to risking his life as a matter of course in his daily job, Corporal Penny volunteered for a particularly hazardous run into the face of strong enemy fire. The fact that he eventually got through and delivered his massages earned him respect from everyone involved, including the senior officers in his regiment. As a result of this brave action he was awarded the Military Medal. The 2¾hp Douglas is seen here as ridden in action, covered in the mud of The Somme. It has several modifications from standard to assist its rider and to improve its performance. There's the big mudshield across the front of the engine for instance, probably custom made in the army workshops, although not helping engine cooling in warm weather. Then there are muffs on the handlebars to protect from spills and to keep the riders hands slightly warmer than they might otherwise be; it all goes to making life that little bit more bearable under the circumstances!
PHOTO HALSGROVE CHS

The Kettering Specials motorcycle section during the 1914-18 war. Amongst the duties of the 'Specials' during the First World War were the instructions to 'safeguard the water supplies from German infiltrators'. They also had to guard vulnerable points, patrol streets and undertake other duties that may have been performed by members of the regular force who had been called up to fight. They played a valuable role in connection with Zeppelin air raids and other acts of war on the civil population. At the beginning of the war when first recruited they were given armbands and decorated truncheons, this was augmented in 1916 by the issue of a proper uniform.

With many of the men off serving in the Great War, it was no unusual sight to see women doing what might have seemed unthinkable a few years previously. To go around collecting orders from customers on a motorcycle, women had to modify their attire quite drastically. Here, Winnie Ashton of Barnstaple wears a long coat, but beneath it there is a good chance that she would be wearing trousers! The little Villiers-engined Sun she is riding would gobble up any trailing skirts, wrapping them around its exposed belt and bringing the machine to a premature stop, and Winnie's modesty to a dramatic crisis. So it was small size boots, gaiters and trousers or there would be no orders...

PHOTO HALSGROVE CHS

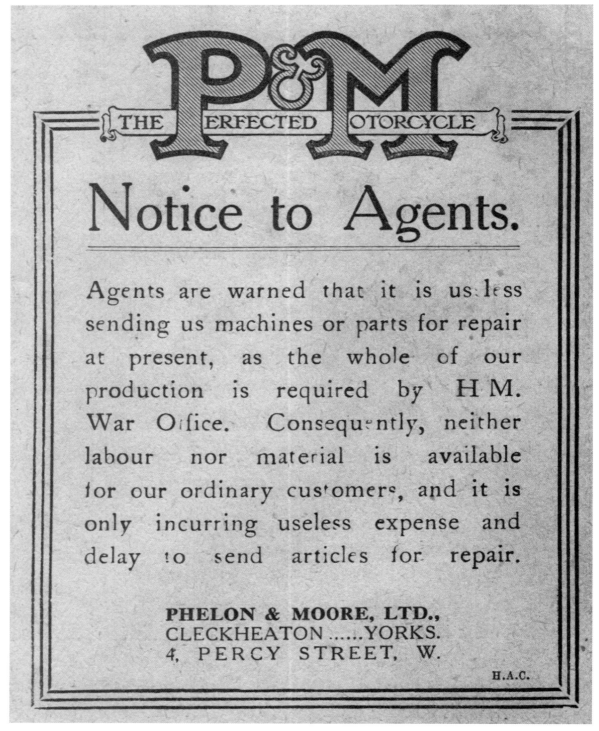

By 1916 most firms had ceased production of motorcycles that were meant purely for civilian use. The firm of Phelon & Moore in Yorkshire devoted their efforts to turning out sidecar machines destined to be used as machine gun carriers and ambulances on the Western Front. Clearly there were quite a lot of their pre-war outfits and solos still being used by private owners, and this advert from 1916 which was put in the weekly motorcycle press stressed the fact that anything other than war work would just have to wait until hostilities were over.

As a direct result of the injuries suffered by so many in the Great War, there were large numbers of disabled servicemen in the early twenties. Seizing the opportunity, several British firms began to manufacture vehicles that could be adapted for limbless men and women for their own personal use. The LAD Company of Farnham marketed a Villiers-engined three wheeler which was just such an

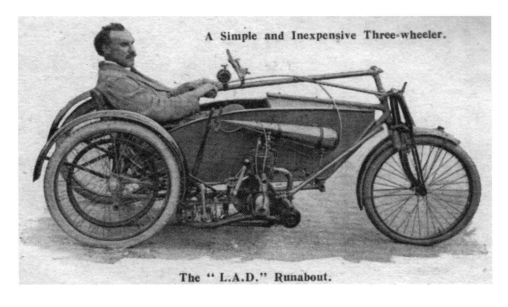

A Simple and Inexpensive Three-wheeler.

The " L.A.D." Runabout.

example. A soldier who had lost the use of his lower limbs could manage their little runabout; there was tiller steering, all necessary controls being mounted conveniently on the handlebars or within easy reach. Handstarting was provided for by the use of the long lever attached in place of a kickstart, and a hand change for the two-speed gearbox bolted directly on to the gearbox itself. Cost was £78 and some, it was reputed, could reach 40 mph!

E A Radnall manufactured motorcycles at their headquarters in Dartmouth Street, Birmingham from before the First World War up to the early thirties. This little photograph shows 'An enthusiastic veteran rider, Mr E Mackburn of Redcar, Yorkshire. He is 82 years of age and is riding his 1919 Radco'. Self styled 'The King of the Lightweights' this is in fact Radco's 2¼hp single-speed Model Number 1. They made their own engine, and a staunch little bike it was too, a correspondent claiming that, even attached to a sidecar it would 'go anywhere'. Radco production halted for a while in 1916, war work was more important, but post war they restarted with a gradual improvement in their two-stroke range, adding a four-stroke JAP engine to their larger bikes in the final years of manufacture. There were any number of these little two strokes about, but the Radco was one of the longer lasting and most efficient of those available.

The garage of C J Frost dealt with the sale and repair of cycles, motorcycles and sometimes cars in the village of Mulbarton, south of Norwich. The owner carries a wrapped up tyre, (they all came bound with string and brown paper when they were new) and forsakes the attentions of a potential customer to smile at the camera. Tyres must have been a good seller for Frosts, as there seem to be lots of them about in the windows and on the floor. Motorcycles

of various sorts are also available, as are second hand and new bicycles from Raleigh and Premier. H Funnell, grocer, baker and confectioner has his Model T delivery van in for a small repair whilst the young apprentice mechanic in his greasy overalls carries a jug. Ah but what was in it, oil or milk for the tea?   PHOTO HALSGROVE CHS

Deep in the heart of Hundred Acre wood, close to the bridge where the game of Pooh Sticks was invented by a small brown bear, a group of motorcyclists gather to play another kind of game in 1919. The riders on motorcycles from the nearby firm of Burney and Blackburne, based in Tongham, Surrey, were engaged on a 'paper chase', the basic rules of which involved them following a trail of torn up paper laid through the countryside by another rider who had already gone on ahead. It is not recorded what A A Milne thought of such activities.

Reg Weeks and his passenger Bill Ablitt on an outing from Ventnor to Calbourne in the Isle of Wight. After the end of the Great War there were a great many army surplus motorcycles about. Returning troops, having learned new skills in the army, which included driving cars and lorries, riding motorcycles and basic mechanical repair and maintenance, wanted their own personal means of transport. Second hand dealers attended auctions of not just vehicles, but also all the other paraphernalia of the armed forces. Waterproof clothing, pilot's hats and goggles, boots, camping equipment, tyres, complete engines, boxes of spark plugs and spanners could all be bought. In this case it looks as if the pair are riding an ex-government 'reconstructed' Triumph. You could get a 4hp 3-speed model from a dealer, say Crabtrees of Wisbech, for £95. They were all advertised as 'being thoroughly overhauled, stove enamelled, replated, tanks in maker's colours, with mostly new tyres and guaranteed mechanically sound'. PHOTO HALSGROVE CHS

1920 – 1929

Powells of St Columb in Cornwall had been established as blacksmiths, carters and hauliers in the late Victorian period. With the coming of the internal combustion engine, they moved with the times and turned their attentions to providing appropriate facilities to support motorists, motorcyclists and others with similar interests. This interesting photo, taken outside their shop around 1920, shows a Model T Ford; and looking through the window you can see a BSA agency sign, and a Baby Triumph for sale. St Columb, near Newquay, had been isolated from the railway when it was built, the town being about three miles away from the nearest station. Powells had bought an old stage coach and ran

regular horse-drawn bus services several times each day to St Columb Road Station. When the coach eventually began to fall to pieces, they took the body off the old cart chassis, and mounted it on the back of this Ford. Look closely and you can still see the coach driver's seat mounted above the cab of the truck.

Below: The sergeant and constable from the Norfolk Constabulary are pictured here outside The Old Police Station at Shadrack Cottage, Litcham Brook, Norfolk. The BSA is a conventional side-valve model from the early twenties. BSA had a very clear market in mind for their motorcycles at the time. They built basic, no frills, machines which got to and from work reliably and dependably. They may not have been capable of winning many races, but they demonstrated their excellence through their exploits in endurance and trials events; ideal for the police and other Government organisations who ordered them from BSA in their thousands. PHOTO HALSGROVE CHS

One of the more unusual trades to use a motorcycle and sidecar was that of travelling beekeeper. Here, Harry Ward of Mill Cottage in Sheringham, Norfolk uses the box sidecar and early 1920s BSA to transport all the things required to keep his bees happy and to collect the honey to sell on to his customers. The wooden bee hives are not so different from those in use nowadays, but the plaited straw version on his rear carrier has long since gone out of general use. PHOTO HALSGROVE CHS

This 1920 ABC 398cc horizontally opposed flat twin was designed and built by Granville Bradshaw. It was a brilliant design, full of novelty and innovation, yet it failed. George Heywood from Plymouth, seen here on his own ABC, was a lifelong devotee of the marque and during his years in the wartime dockyards managed to collect several examples. The ABC had rear springing, a car-style gate gearchange with four speeds and clutch, dynamo electric lighting and a black crackle finish. Its best modern comparison is the LE Velocette, and on paper at least it was difficult to fault it. However it cost £160, you could buy three '250's' for that at the time. Top speed was around 60mph, although one of its recurring faults apparently was the ejection of loose-fitting push rods, usually over the hedge and into the next field. BMW benefitted from the design, as did the French Gnome & Rhone Company. It was an engineer's bike; the untapped market of the man in the street finally eluded it.

Inez Trenerry lived near Helston in Cornwall and was a keen motorist and motorcyclist. The 1922 Sun she is riding here had a 350cc JAP side-valve engine. Other models in the Sun range provided AZA, Blackburne, and Villiers engines as an alternative means of powering their machines. Possibly provoking some comments from onlookers, Inez rode her Sun most days to and from work. Mounted on the headlight is a little mascot, one of many such items that could be bought at garages or gift shops ready to clip on to handlebars or car radiator grills. PHOTO HALSGROVE CHS

Fernley 'Swifty' Warne, born in 1888, was a water bailiff who lived in the middle of Dartmoor, not far from Princetown. A water bailiff is charged with enforcing laws relating to salmon and trout. They are not police officers, but do have powers of entry, seizure and arrest. This gentleman would have been on the look out for illegal poaching activities in and around the many rivers which flow down from the moors to the sea. It is also quite likely that he would have been involved in the sport of otter hunting which peaked in this country in the pre Great War years. His little bike is of an unknown make but representative of the many lightweight machines with Villiers engines that were turned out in their thousands to provide transport for the newly demobbed soldiers. Swifty was very gadget-conscious and has equipped his steed with all kinds of extras; look at the mirrors, the klaxon horn, the big gas lights and the speedometer. It couldn't have done much for his off road capabilities though, and speed in pursuit of any villains would have been cut by several miles and hour. PHOTO HALSGROVE CHS

This picture of J Bance on his 1922 Blackburne shows what the up-to-date racing motorcyclist was wearing for his own protection. Although speeds were relatively slow by modern standards, the roads were primitive, the bikes were built for speed and the combination of the two meant frequent spills. The rider's helmet is a kind of Bakelite covered in leather with little rolls of leather around the ears to keep the goggle strap in position. The leather jacket was buttoned up, no zips then, and the trousers were Jodhpur style, most inelegant when walking but seemingly comfortable when adopting a prone racing position. Long lace up boots and thick hide gloves completed the ensemble. Look closely though, and see how many gaps the wind could find to whistle through; up the arms, past the buttons on the chest, and in through the flies. Perhaps Mr Bance needed the coffee on offer at the public refreshments stall in the background. This was a swan song for Blackburne motorcycles; although they continued for many years making proprietary engines, they ceased manufacturing complete machines in the year the photo was taken. Mr Bance finished 9th in the 1922 350cc Junior TT, 42 minutes after the winner Tom Sheard on an AJS.

Opposite: Many of the motorcycle companies that were based in Birmingham used the local countryside to test their bikes. Sunrising Hill, near Banbury was a famous test hill; if your machine could get up the steep escarpment at Edge Hill with its hairpin curves then it had to be performing reasonably well. Similarly, long-distance trials were also used to test the machine's capabilities. This route card from a 1922 24-hour trial for bikes and cars, maps out an overnight run from Birmingham to North Wales and back. Machines had to be 'weighed in', a term borrowed from the horse racing fraternity, and if passed as fit were required to start in the gathering gloom of a summer's evening. Through the night they rode, and on the way had to do a lot of 'tests' on old lanes, in the dark. North Wales was another important testing ground for the Birmingham manufacturers, and a timed and observed ascent of Bwlch-y-Groes was a favourite amongst riders and the general public.

The Midland Cycling & Athletic Club
AND
The Midland Car Club,
Joint 24 Hour Trial, July 7th & 8th, 1922.

First Man.	Your Time.	DIRECTIONS.	Intermediate Distances	Total Miles.	Grand Total.
7 0	7.48	START from Sansome Davis Garage, Stratford Road, Robin Hood.	0	0	0
7 1	7.49	Shirley, 1st R. and in 1 mile R fork, then follow Telegraph Wires to Maypole on Alcester Road, turn R and follow to	⅓	⅓	
7 9	7.57	Mill Pool Hill. WEIGH-IN. L at bottom, and joining Road with Tel. Wires follow to Top of Parsons Hill, descend to	2⅔	3	
7 16	8.4	Rubery New... ... Valley Green turn R.	2¼	5¼	
		At S.P. to... bridge turn R.			
7 29	8.11	Longbridge turn L on to Main Road and R over bridge.	2⅓	7⅔	
7 39	8.27	Bromsgrove, R Fork by Clock, S.P. to	5½	13	
8 9	8.57	Kidderminster, straight through on Road to	10	23	
8 51	9.39	Bridgnorth, L over River Bridge then R fork up Hill to High Town, L near end S.P. to Shrewsbury.	14	37	
9 14	10.2	Much Wenlock, L at bottom of Hill into village, R past Bridge	7⅔	44⅔	
		Cressage, L in village. **Non-Stop**			
9 48	10.36	Shrewsbury. TIME CHECK at Lo... Hill Monument. Proceed into centre of Town turn R for Raven Garage.	11⅓	56	56
		Supper at Boots Café Pride Hill.			
11 0	11.48	Shrewsbury. Leave via Welsh Bridge and take R fork ½ miles beyond town.	0	0	56
11 39	12.27	Queen's Head take R fork.	13	13	
		Whittington.			
12 3	12.51	Chirk.			
12 24	1.12	Llangollen.	7	28	
12 54	1.42	Corwen.	10	38	
		Cerrig-y-Druidion.			
2 0	2.48	Bettws-y-Coed, L over Waterloo Bridge and then R beyond Station. *Keep River on your R to*	22	60	
2 51	3.39	Conway.	17	77	
3 33	4.21	Bangor, in High Street turn R along Farrar Road follow to Holyhead Road.	14	91	
3 42	4.30	Menai Bridge (Have change ready for Toll).	3	94	
4 45	5.33	Holyhead. TIME CHECK at the Holyhead Motor Co., Kingsland Road.	21	115	171
		Breakfast at the Station Hotel.			
6 0	6.48	Holyhead.	0	0	
7 3	7.51	Menai Bridge, after crossing Bridge turn R for	21	21	
7 21	8.9	Carnarvon.	6	27	
7 42	8.30	Llanberis, R after Castle Hotel, then 1st R & 1st L	7	34	
		Cefn-Du. OBSERVED.			
		Groeslon, L for			
7 54	8.42	Waen-fawr, L on Main Road for	4	38	
8 21	9.9	Beddgelert.	9	47	
8 42	9.30	Penrhyn-deudraeth. (Have change ready for Toll)	7	54	
9 0	9.48	Harlech. TIME CHECK. **Non-Stop**	6	60	
		Barmouth.	11	71	
		Llanelltyd, turn R over River.	7	78	
10 0	10.48	Dolgelley.	2	80	
		Cross Foxes Inn.	3	83	
10 30	11.18	Dinas Mawddwy. TIME CHECK, through village to **Non-stop**	7	90	
		Bwlch-y-Groes. TIMED & OBSERVED.			
		Descending Hill L for			
		Llanuwchllyn. R on Main Road to			
11 27	12.15	Bala. TIME CHECK. **Non-Stop**	18	108	279

The insignia of King George V on the side of this box sidecar in 1921 indicates a postman making his delivery, in this case to a rural location near Wincanton. Before the First World War the Post Office had experimented with the use of motorcycles to replace postmen on horseback in more remote communities. The war, along with its attendant petrol shortages, had curtailed these trials, but after hostilities had ceased, motorcycling was resumed, but this time with more powerful machines for the postmen. The Post Office bought a variety of makes to try out on the rounds; Matchless, BSA, Triumph, Enfield, Douglas, Clyno and Chater Lea were all assessed under a variety of conditions and circumstances. In the end BSA proved to be the best in terms of price and quality, and won the contract to be the suppliers. This continued for a number of years, and the bike illustrated here is indeed a BSA. PHOTO HALSGROVE CHS

Below: The employees of Trumps Stores are lined up outside the shop in Broad Street, Ottery St Mary, in the early twenties for a staff photograph. The vehicles parked in front of the shop all worked together in harmony, each having their uses. The vans, Model T Ford included, would obviously tackle the bigger orders, whilst the horses might do more local trips. The horses were in fact being phased out, but being rather sentimental Trumps still held on to and employed them for old time's sake. The motorcycle combination took groceries around the town, and it also did the rounds to the more outlying Devon villages such as Payhembury and Buckrell. PHOTO HALSGROVE CHS

The building firm of Chidgey & Morse who worked out of Watchet in Somerset are seen here transporting their men to work in the mid twenties. Most of the workmen are in the back of the solid-tyred Thornycroft X type three-ton lorry, but one, carrying his sandwiches on his back, is riding a Triumph Model H. This was the time of the General Strike and Great Depression when workers would often be employed on an irregular daily basis, it was a time of uncertainty and low wages and you were lucky if you could afford to keep a motorbike on the road at the time. PHOTO HALSGROVE CHS

Grindlay Peerless successes at Brooklands were largely due to the efforts of their consistently successful rider, Bill Lacey. Their machines were beautifully prepared with all bright parts nickeled and highly polished. Lacey was engaged to Miss Mae Ruffel, who was herself an excellent rider. This photograph of Miss Ruffel, later Mrs Lacey, shows her winning the Wakefield cup on a 1928 350cc Grindlay when she reached 79.78mph. With gear lever firmly wedged in top, compulsory

Brooklands Can on upside down, and a wet bottom from the lack of mudguards, Mae Ruffel adopts a racing crouch as she thunders along Hangar Straight. PHOTO J VICKERS

Like so many other manufacurers BSA produced bicycles, but they also produced guns and other industrial machines and tools from their Small Heath factory. Being in close proximity to the railways and canals, the firm used these as a means of transporting their goods and bringing in raw materials, often in preference to the long road journeys to their farther flung dealerships. This lovely 1927 photo demonstrates how important horses still were, even to a company which manufactured motorised vehicles. The special container, holding fifty bicycles, was one of a number dispatched from the Works to agents in various parts of the country in readiness for the summer holidays.

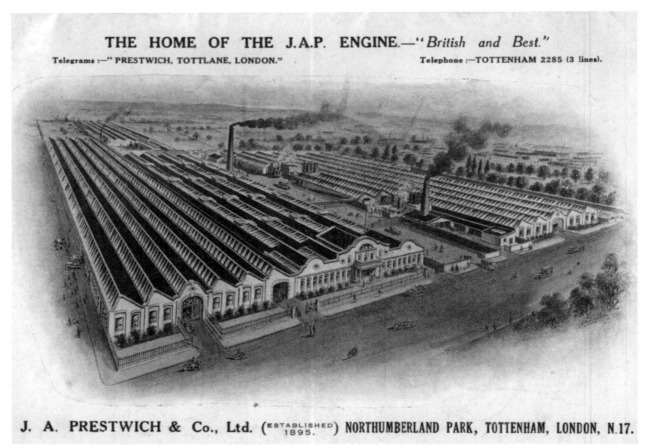

THE HOME OF THE J.A.P. ENGINE.—"British and Best."

Telegrams :—" PRESTWICH, TOTTLANE, LONDON."   Telephone :—TOTTENHAM 2285 (3 lines).

J. A. PRESTWICH & Co., Ltd. (ESTABLISHED 1895.) NORTHUMBERLAND PARK, TOTTENHAM, LONDON, N.17.

To an old time motorcyclist the letters JAP can only have one meaning, they are the initials of the founder of one of Britain's most iconic manufacturers of engines; John Alfred Prestwich. Initially Prestwich was interested in the newly emerging cinematograph industry, and he produced projectors, cameras, printers and the like. But he was also working within the infant automotive industry, and made his own motorcycles from 1904 to 1908. JAP engines became very popular for use by other motorcycle makers, and they were also used in aircraft; A.V.Roe's 1909 triplane used one for instance. From his factory in Tottenham, pictured in this 1930 brochure, Prestwich steadily developed his engines to the point where they were used in all kinds of settings. The big V-twins were put into Morgans and Broughs, singles were put into a whole plethora of British and European marques, many of them for sporting and record breaking use. There were also smaller engines designed as the motive power in rotavators, water pumps, mowers and so on. Eventually the JAP factory closed in 1963 and manufacture of engines was taken over by Villiers.

Godfreys
Guide
to trouble-free
motoring for
1928

With Compliments from
GODFREYS LIMITED
208, GREAT PORTLAND STREET, W.1
366 - 368, EUSTON ROAD, N.W.1
232, STAMFORD HILL, N.16

Supporting the motorcycle industry was a whole raft of accessory manufacturers and distributors. One such example was Godfreys of London who provided 'an interesting handbook of helpfulness to all who would enjoy the freedom of the country'. You could buy a brand new bike from them, but they would also sell you secondhand machines or spares. There were other items seductively laid out in their catalogue to tempt the rider with a few bob to spend; a speedometer, waterproof leggings, puncture repair outfits and wonder polish. They encouraged overseas customers with tables showing charges for packing, freight and insurance to ports in different parts of the world, and had an extended payment plan if you wished to take advantage of that. Everything needed to get on the road was available here at Godfreys in 1928!

Below: 'Young' Ernest Honey sits with his dog at Fenterwanson near Camelford in Cornwall on his 1928 557cc Model B Ariel. Ariels were very publicity conscious at the time, and pulled off some spectacular stunts. On an overhead-valve version of this bike they managed to attach it to a sort of seaplane float, with the rear wheel driving a propeller through bevel gears. They managed to get it to cross the English Channel in just under four hours, although apparently the sea bed was strewn with dropped Ariel spanners. Ernest's father was also the owner of a motorcycle, and worked at the nearby De Lank slate quarry. One day, whilst returning home with a bunch of wild flowers called 'grannys bonnets' for his wife, Mr Honey (senior) was involved in a fatal accident very close to where this picture was taken.

'This is the Norton and sidecar Father bought and which he used for his deliveries around Northlew on the edge of Dartmoor. We had to keep stopping to replace the silencer which was always falling off, and we couldn't stay out after dark because the jets in the acetylene lights kept blocking up.' During the twenties Nortons had consolidated their enviable reputation for reliability and build quality with their racing successes. However they continued to build machines for the masses, including specially designed models which would cope with heavy sidecars. The single cylinder side-valve Big Four, an example of which is shown here, was first introduced in 1907, and with continual development was still around well into the fifties. PHOTO HALSGROVE CHS

'Good news for all those who are thinking about motorcycles, for the new 4.98hp Raleigh is ready for delivery, only in small numbers at present, but those whose names are at the top of the list will soon own this fine machine with all the very latest improvements in motor-cycle design. If you are looking for something right up to date and for a machine that will be a leader in its class, send in your name now and we will put you in touch with the nearest Raleigh Dealer. 1926 Prices; £45 or £11-5s down and 12 monthly payments of £3 11s 6d.' Wonder which payment Jim Hodges chose? He is seen here with passenger Eddie Pither at Winsgrave, Malvern.
PHOTO HALSGROVE CHS

'Just sold the push bike and got this Triumph, and felt I had to show it off to a group of my chums. Of course they all want to have a good look and see how fast it will go. The least I could do was let them sit on it and have their picture taken'. The range of Triumph side-valves, like this SD model, was based on the successes they had with their despatch riders' bikes in the Great War. To bring it up to date they fitted a three-speed gearbox and used a chain instead of a belt for the final drive. Could do with a bit of air in the back tyre though! This is Budleigh Salterton around 1930. PHOTO HALSGROVE CHS

Below: The Radco company were keen on entering their machines in competitions, but these tended to be trials or stock machine events rather than out-and-out races. Still there were certain private owners who bought the late twenties ohv Jap engined models and had a go, and were in part supported by the factory. Here at the French TT of 1928, P G Dallison is entered on his Radco and is seen on what appears to be a stripped down standard 490cc ohv model. The road test in 1928 suggested that the bike was heavy but provided a feeling of power and an ability to stand up to any amount of hard usage, ideal properties for the tough conditions of the TT races.

'Once a Bif (Bristol Fighter) flew over and I waved.....the pilot pointed down the straight road...I sat hard in the saddle, folded back my ears and went after him like a dog after a hare'. T E Lawrence wrote one of the most compelling and dramatic accounts of the race on his Brough Superior 'Boanerges' against the aircraft from a neighbouring airfield. Lawrence, of course won the race, being faster than the fighter by around 5mph, and having to wait for the most modern of the RAF's aircraft to catch him up. Perhaps Dad taking these two children to school has this incident in mind, then again he may just be late for the train. A nice original, unsigned watercolour painting.

Everybody thinks that their bike is best, but curiosity means that you have to try another similar machine, just to see what its like compared with your own. Triumph produced large volumes of bikes in the late twenties, and here we have a swap going on. At Hatch Bridge near Loddiswell, Henry Eastley on Bert Elliot's Triumph and Jack Hyne on his own version try to work out which is superior. There was a drastic rationalisation of models at Triumph in 1928, only four models were offered, and the two side-valve engined machines pictured here were based on the updated Model P introduced in 1925. They were fairly conventional, with some suspect parts, like the brakes, big-end bearings and front brake, but still they sold well at prices as low as £35 if you shopped around. In the event, the test was inconclusive, both models' performance being very similar to one another.
PHOTO HALSGROVE CHS

Below: The High Street in Honiton was well served by garages, hotels and petrol stations, all built to serve passing travellers as well as the local trade. This was, after all, the main A30 road from London to Devon and Cornwall. It was still a small rural town in 1926 when this photo was taken, and the roads and pavements were not well suited to the demands of modern traffic. The petrol pumps of Moor's Garage for instance needed to have long gantries mounted above the shop so that the pipes could reach across the pavement to the vehicles that needed refills. Moor's was agent for Rudge Whitworth, but also carried out repairs and was recognised by both the AA and RAC. Waiting beside the Bullnose Morris Oxford, the three motorcycles include a big 1000cc Model H Matchless sidecar outfit of around 1920.   PHOTO HALSGROVE CHS

The state of many rural roads in the mid twenties was in much the same condition as they had been one hundred years before. The process of macadaming, that is the piling of small stones on top of larger ones to make a firm road bed, then rolling them in, had been started in Victorian times, but the addition of tar as a binding agent only became widespread in the early part of the twentieth century. Improvements to all roads continued, but the less-well-used rural byways were quite a long way down the list and this, together with the number of animals which still used them on a daily basis meant that it was often very difficult to get around when it had been raining hard. The road between Stoke Abbott and Beaminster in Dorset was used by the local farmer to drive his cows along, and Mr C Smith thought he would have no difficulty getting his Model P Triumph outfit along it too, but in the event he encountered a few problems! PHOTO HALSGROVE CHS

Below: Horace Dunstan, milk purveyor of Goonlaze Dairy, Stithians, near Redruth, delivering to his customers in the late twenties. BSA sidecar outfits seemed to be very much the favourite amongst dairymen for this job! Watsonian made two types of sidecar for commercial purposes in 1928. The 'Box' was suitable for most trades for the transportation of small parcels, it could carry up to three hundredweight and could be supplied with a 'Kwikfit' chassis, enabling it to be removed in one minute. Their open-topped 'Truck' was suitable for farmers, dairymen, builders and other similar trades. The standard size would accommodate two milk churns, but the company would also quote for special requirements. PHOTO HALSGROVE CHS

This milkman and the BSA with the young family aboard are from Sennen, within a mile or so of Land's End. It was not easy to access mass markets when selling milk from remote farms. The nearest big town to Sennen is Penzance, nearly ten miles away, and the milk factory would have been at St Erth, another ten miles beyond. Although there were lorries which could come around to the farms to collect and return churns it was more profitable and convenient to not only to find someone locally to buy the milk, but also to transport it to them yourself. There was probably enough tourist and passing trade even at the time this photograph was taken in the thirties to make it a worthwhile exercise for the farmer.
PHOTO HALSGROVE CHS

We are pretty sure that Mr Burgess, owner of this bakery and confectionery shop in Porlock Vale was not just someone who used his BSA as an everyday workhorse. We know for instance that he could change the body at weekends for a different coach-built model for the family to travel in, and we presume that he must have had an interest in the sporting side of two- and four-wheeled vehicles because his daughters were encouraged to spectate on the hillclimbs just up the road at Porlock Hill. Porlock would have presented few problems to Mr Burgesses 8hp V-twin BSA, they were all thoroughly tested up such inclines as Screw Hill in the Lleyn Peninsula and at Bwylch-y-Groes near Bala. Mr Burgess may well have bought his combination on the strength of the advertising that came from these publicity efforts. PHOTO HALSGROVE CHS

Below: Lisles Garage at Woolmer Green, Herts, in the mid twenties with a full collection of motorcycles, trucks, cars and even a cart. The garage was started in 1900 by William Lisle as an engineering and motor repair establishment, and later sold petrol and oil from its forecourt. 'Fill up here with Shell' says the sign on the mobile petrol dispenser, whilst the early petrol pump seems slightly vulnerable on its little concrete island. The mobile dispenser was in effect just a great big bucket with petrol sloshing about inside, and only a lid for protection. Palmer and Dunlop Tyres could be supplied, and the Vacuum Mobiloil enamel sign with its gargoyle logo dates from the early part of the century when the garage was first established. PHOTO HALSGROVE CHS

The forge at Bury, Dulverton on Exmoor, is the scene of this encounter between cow and motorcycle. It's often forgotten that until quite recently domestic cows had long horns. The horns were never removed, and although they did represent something of a hazard, generally there were few problems in the everyday running of the farm. The motorcycle is quite rare, being a flat twin 700cc 5-6hp Raleigh from around 1920. Raleigh in their adverts for this model asked why the demand for Raleigh was already so great. Why had they been compelled to make great factory extensions? Their answer was that they had spent thousands of pounds in perfecting it before it went on sale to the public. In fact this model only lasted until 1924 when the flat twin was replaced by a more conventional V-twin of their own manufacture. PHOTO HALSGROVE CHS

There is to be a wedding in the small Devon village beneath the rolling hills of Dartmoor. The bride's Mother wears her best church dress, no coat is necessary because it's a beautiful day and the hat will blow off if she puts it on anyway. The bridegroom sits on the back of the family BSA whilst the father with the rose in his buttonhole prepares to make the short journey down the lane to the church. It is high summer in 1926, the garden is full of fruit and vegetables, the wild flowers are out in the hedgerows and the birds are singing. It is going to be a very memorable day, so better take a few snaps for the family album.

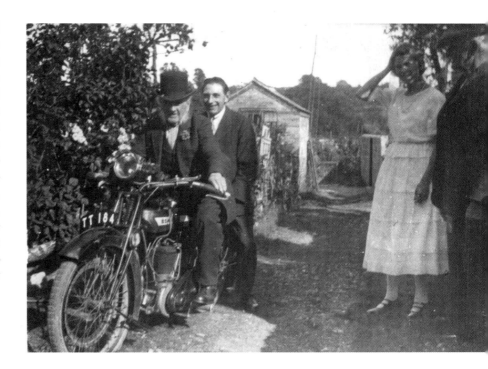

Calder Farm, near Ravensthorpe in Northamptonshire had been established in 1855 as a reformatory school for boys who had committed acts of petty theft. It had a strict regime, but was said to have provided a much better standard of living than the boys might have expected in their own homes. It closed in 1922 as a school. There would have been much emphasis on practical working skills, the boys having to learn such things as gardening, farming and other manual trades as appropriate. Here the school's sidecar outfit is seen on the gravel track outside Calder Farm, the chickens in their runs would have supplied food for the school and would also have provided a useful learning experience for the boys.

Below: Peter Bradley eases his 1929 Sunbeam down into the stream on a cold and wet winter's day in a Midland Trial. There is snow in the air, the lanes are muddy and his passenger Bert Tetsall wonders whether this is another of those 'get out and push me out of here please?' moments. Bradley has taken his gloves off, so he must mean business!

THE JOYS OF THE OPEN ROAD.

Postcards of a bawdy nature were always popular, the prime illustrator and most well known being Donald McGill. This example, although not Mcgill's, was aimed at the 'two wheel brigade on holiday' market. Sales were quite lucrative; it seems that there are many such cards which have survived, so hundreds of thousands must have been bought. Written on the back in pencil is a cryptic message from Dolly to Freddie saying 'well you couldn't help it, girls fall off the d... byke in front of you'.

Below: The Massey Arran team entered the 1921 TT races in the Isle of Man with great expectations. Jim Whalley, seen here, did in fact lead the race for a while; however in the last lap he punctured his rear tyre at Windy Corner, crashing heavily and damaging his gear control and several other items. He managed to restart, but could not change gear so, stuck in second, with the rear tyre hanging off the rim and holding the exhaust pipe in position and with blood pouring from his wounds he managed to get to the Grandstand where he finished fifth. Howard Davies on an AJS was the eventual winner. However, it's a fair bet that if there had been a competition to see which team owned the biggest dog then perhaps Mr Whalley might have been the winner with this massive Great Dane.

Opposite, top: This photograph is labelled 'Charles in front of the packing sheds at Sawley Villa, Blofield circa 1924'. Blofield is a village in Norfolk, and there was a lot of horticultural and agricultural activity in the area, the packing sheds being part of that industry. The unknown bike is another one of the innumerable makes that were turned out after the Great War. Some of these little two strokes were produced by large factories trying to keep going after their war work dried up, others were constructed in a back shed by two-men-and-a-boy outfits. As long as you had a bit of pipe and an engine, you were away! There was even one machine made at the time, the Edmund, which was sold without a name; you could buy it and simply put your own transfer on it and say that you had manufactured it yourself. Charles' two-wheeler has a Villiers engine, with a big flywheel to keep up its momentum and is a single-speed belt-driven machine. There was no clutch or gearbox, you just peddled away for a few yards, released the decompressor and off you went. PHOTO HALSGROVE CHS

Opposite, bottom left: The Ner-a Car appeared in 1921 and was immediately recognised as being something rather unusual. The name stems from a double pun, the designer was named Neracher, and it was supposed to be 'near a car' in looks. It had a car-like chassis with pivoted forks providing suspension at either end, although most of this was hidden beneath an enormous and all-enveloping mudguard so that the model could be ridden in ordinary clothes. The drive of this early two stroke version was by friction, the flywheel drove an aluminium disc, faced with fibre and positioned at right angles to it, which in turn was connected to the rear wheel by a chain. There were five notches on the gear lever, so five different ratios. It was described as being skid-proof due to its very low centre of gravity, and was supposedly most useful to professional women living in country, districts-midwives, village organists etc. This group of three include 'June Thomas, Mr Brammer and myself' and was taken by the unknown camerawoman in July 1927.

Opposite, bottom right: Arthur Thorn of Monksilver in North Somerset owned a 1921 OK Junior motorcycle, and dressed in style when he rode it. OK Juniors were made by the firm of Humphries & Dawes in Birmingham. They had been in business since 1899 making motorcycles, and in 1910 adopted the name 'OK Junior' for their range of two-wheeled products. By 1914 a range of three, single cylinder, machines was being offered to the public using their own engines. There was a 296cc fixed gear model for £27.5s, a 190cc chain-cum-belt version for £36.15s and a similar cycle but with a 292cc engine for £38. Production continued right up to 1916, when it stopped because of the continuing war. Arthur is riding one of the pre-war versions; OK re-emerged after the war to become OK Supreme and manufactured a variety of motorcycles right up to 1940. PHOTO HALSGROVE CHS

Below: Raleigh was inaugurated in 1887 as a bicycle manufacturing company by Mr Frank Bowden. Most people associate the name Bowden with the wire control cables which he patented in 1894, however his high-grade bicycles, and later motorcycles were of the highest quality. They were sometimes a little unimaginative, but were made of the finest possible materials, whilst their plating and paintwork left little to be desired. Raleigh spent a lot of money on advertising their products; they did a variety of publicity stunts and in the late twenties ran a successful racing team. However their motorcycles never seemed to enjoy the share of the market that was due to them, and customers viewed the machines as merely utilitarian rather than objects of desire. Arthur Jenkins is sitting on a 1929 350cc side-valve 'Raleigh', although strictly speaking this was a firm that was by then owned by the Sturmey Archer concern. PHOTO HALSGROVE CHS

Stella Shear, the glamorous young lady in the centre of the picture lived in the village of Sticker, near St Austell in Cornwall. In the early thirties her brother in law, Herbie, owned the 1925 side-valve AJS shown here. Herbie lived a long life and his interest in motorcycles never faded. He was for many years a bit of a dealer, buying and selling old bikes. He never got interested in Japanese stuff, dismissing it all with contempt. Stella's husband, Tom, started a haulage business in the village which continues to this day under the leadership of his son Charles. The dog's name is not recorded. PHOTO HALSGROVE CHS

The OK Supreme Company had developed after the Great War into a company that made a range of motorcycles using not just their own engines, but also those supplied by Blackburne and JAP. The Prestwich engines were then used exclusively from 1926 onwards. There was a range of between six and ten models available during the thirties which had wonderful names like 'Britannia', 'Flying Cloud', 'Hood' and 'Phantom'. Bill Rice's machine shown here

at Witheridge in Devon has a JAP engine and Sturmey Archer gearbox. It dates from around 1930, and includes extras such as electric lighting and speedometer. He obviously carries a pillion passenger; the inflatable rubber cushion on the rear carrier was available from all good accessory shops at the time and considerably added to the comfort of the occupant. PHOTO HALSGROVE CHS

Above left: There always seems to be a group of people who want to overload their motorcycle. This little gang of youngsters on their Indian is a typical example. Indians had a good reputation for their advanced engineering and performance, having a history of racing successes in the Isle of Man, Brooklands, and at other competitive events both in this country and in the United States, their homeland. The 1000cc V-twin Powerplus pictured here was about eight years old when this photograph was taken on 10 July 1923 at the home of the Polkinhorne family in Bodmin, Cornwall; it may even have been a war surplus machine.

Above right: 'Daddy on his scooter'. A photograph from the mid twenties shows this slightly apprehensive looking gentleman on his Kingsbury scooter. The aftermath of the Great War led to a surge in demand for personal transport, and resulted in, amongst other mechanical contrivances, the scooter; and the Kingsbury is literally that, a child's scooter with an engine. The original models had no seat, you scooted along, let the decompressor out, and the engine started if you were lucky. Top speed was around 15mph, despite the fact that it had a 225cc engine. The handlebars were the only things to hang on to, and progression was in a series of weaves until you got used to its peculiar handling. There was no suspension and although there were two brakes, they both worked on the rear wheel. Despite the seat fitted to this later version, the rider looks quite content to stay where he is, rather than venture out on to the highway!

Below: This Triumph from the mid twenties is capable of carrying a pillion, something which perhaps ten or fifteen years before would not have been the case. Before the Great War the carrying of passengers suspended over the rear mudguard was not acceptable; magazines warned that it was as 'dangerous as flying an aircraft'. Outraged citizens wrote letters

deploring the fact that young ladies' thighs could be made out beneath their dresses, demands were even made that men with female pillionists should be made to produce their marriage licence before proceeding. After the war common sense prevailed, manufacturers produced a great range of suitably sprung and fully-anchored saddles and this, combined with a fashionable change of clothing styles, eventually put and end to the old attitude. There was a demand however for a fitment that could be attached to the rear carrier and which allowed the lady to ride side saddle, as opposed to astride the bike, and here we have such an example.

Collins & Carr's Motor Cycle and Cycle Repair Depot was attached to the Parkwood Garage in Tavistock. It's clear from the picture what their business involved, so it is interesting to look in detail at what was going on here in 1926 when the photo was taken. The line up of motorcycles for sale includes a Sunbeam, a James, a New Imperial, a Douglas and what is probably a Kenilworth scooter which is just visible behind the Douglas. The car, an American Durant, which is in for repair has an old Devon trade plate on it. They sold Pratt's Perfection Motor Spirit, and there was a choice of oils from Shell, Royal Daylight, BP and Pratt's. They were agents for James motorcycles and also BSA

cycles. Messrs Collins & Carr were keen to promote the sporting side of motorcycling because in the window, alongside the big display featuring James motorcycles, is an advert for some forthcoming local speed trials. There is a clear demarcation in the dress code of the members of staff. Owners and salesmen had ties and suits, whilst mechanics, petrol pump attendants and apprentices wore boiler suits and more workaday attire, twas ever thus!

PHOTO HALSGROVE CHS

Above: Posing outside the shop in Williton near Taunton there are a group of gentlemen who are mechanics, perhaps friends or just general onlookers. Mr Bradbeer lived above his workplace which not only sold cars and motorcycles but also repaired them and sold Pratt's petrol to refuel them. It was one of those curious things about garages in the twenties that they also seemed to sell a lot of things to do with the newly-emerging radio and recording industry. Certainly 78rpm records had been around for some time, and what was becoming a much more widespread use of the radio, principally with the emergence of 2LO and the BBC, encouraged establishments like garages to diversify into that area. Presumably the thinking was that if you could fix a car, you could also get a wireless to work properly, and of course these establishments also had the facilities for recharging the wet cell batteries used by many radios at that time. Did the mechanics prefer working on the Austin Sevens or the little round tank BSA one wonders?
PHOTO HALSGROVE CHS

Opposite, top: The Land's End Trial, held each Easter weekend by the Motor Cycling Club, has been going since 1908. It is essentially a reliability test of man and machine, originally going from London to Land's End and back through the night, and for motorcycles only. In 1914 light cars were permitted to enter, and in 1920 all types of cars could have a go. This group of riders is at Portreath on the north Cornish coast in 1926. They are facing uphill on a road which still exists but is no longer a through-route due to an airfield, RAF Nancekuke, having been built across its path. Matchless, AJS and Panther machines can be spotted. Behind the beach the steep road which follows the cliffs along to Hayle begins with a right hand bend which is often covered with drifting sand. It remains a formidable challenge to riders of older motorcycles, belt-driven machines really struggle to get up, the alternative being to turn round and go back to Redruth, a diversion of five miles or so.

Opposite, bottom: In 1926, what is now the A386 at Lydford was not much more than a dusty country lane. Little used except by local traffic, much of it still horse drawn, it was a place where you could have a sit on your grandfather's sidecar and freewheel up and down, just to see how it felt. The boy is astride a 348cc EW Douglas which was brand new at the time. The EW was a good reliable mount, The Douglas trials team achieved success after success with it. The gear change through the centre of the tank is unusual, and compactness of the side-valve engine allows the gearbox to be mounted behind it. For £14 Douglas offered their specially designed lightweight sidecar for the 348cc model, or a heavier version for the larger 600cc EW. PHOTO HALSGROVE CHS

During the nineteen twenties there existed a great infrastructure of railways. If you broke down on your motorcycle it was easy to push the bike to a local station and get it home by train. Similarly, if you wanted a new bike then often deliveries were made by rail. This group of Douglas machines has just arrived outside the local station and is being picked up to take back to the shop. The workhorse for this particular job is an old Matchless with a 'float' on to which the brand new bikes can be loaded. The Douglas machines, priced at £41.10s are 1927 EW models, and come complete with their gas lights. The EW was a 3.48hp, three-speed, all chain drive machine, whilst the 1924 Matchless used as the 'Hack' was powered by a big 1000cc engine designed for sidecar use.

Haskin's shop was at 14 City Road, St Paul's right in the centre of Bristol. This photograph, taken not long after the end of the Great War, shows the range and volume of the machines he could supply. Always there were a lot of low-powered machines for sale, one example which can be made out is the little Levis Popular at the end of the row. Mr Haskin's ghostly image peers out from the window, just to the left of his price lists. This area of Bristol was badly damaged during the Blitz, but the address can still be found.

Long distance reliability trials were a big thing before the war, and were keenly contested by both ordinary clubmen and factory riders. The exact location of this ford is not known, however it is providing the spectators with much entertainment. Older bikes often had their magneto stuck out in front of the engine, making them vulnerable to water. There was a real art in the waterproofing of a mag so that it could survive a submersion such as the one illustrated above. Plenty of grease was lagged around the cover and the HT lead, you could buy special Lodge waterproof plugs; plasticene also played a significant role. It worked for some, but not all. The unfortunate stalled rider could be forced to dismount mid stream and push on to dry land. The fun then was to try and find a dry rag to soak up all the excess water, although if you did it quickly enough the warmth from the still hot engine could assist the drying off process.

Round Tank BSAs were pretty simple machines with a basic side-valve engine, two-speed gearbox, both brakes acting on the back wheel and not a lot else to go wrong. Cecil and Len Murton are seen here investigating one in Haughley Green near Stowmarket around 1929, trying to find out why it wouldn't go. 'First, has it got petrol?

Then has it got a spark? Take out the plug and kick it over. Is the petrol getting through to the carb? If it's got all that, then the thing has just got to start. It may be the answer is to give it a push, the mixture may be a bit rich and the kick start just isn't man enough to turn the engine over fast enough. If that doesn't work then get it up on the bench and we'll have a proper go at the mag and carb, perhaps try a new plug'.

PHOTO HALSGROVE CHS

73

It was the place to be seen during 'Wakes Week'; Blackpool could provide for all your needs. The B&B with the same friendly landladies, the beach, the trams, the amusements. The Tower just had to be visited and a ride on a donkey was a must. Souvenirs had to bought; sticks of rock, cuddly toys and ash trays with seagulls. And just to remind you of the grand time that you had, and to give you something to look forward to next year, what not have a photograph taken? Many photographers had their studios on the prom, and they all had their own props and backgrounds. It's surprising how many chose motorcycles as a feature for their portrait backdrop, there seem to be hundreds of surviving postcards showing families, individuals or groups posing with a two wheeler. It does say something for the status of even a humble motorcycle that they should be socially acceptable enough to fulfil this role. Here a pair of modern young ladies drape themselves over a side-valve Grindlay Peerless against the rustic background of an English country church. Ah, memories!

'Getting ready for the hols'. This lovely little painting taken from an unknown book illustrates a boy's image of motorcycling in the late twenties. Without knowing the story which it is supposed to illustrate, it's not difficult to give it a scenario. The two minor public schoolboys, coming up to the end of term at their boarding school, cannot wait to get the old iron, manufactured by The Plough engineering company, out of the bike sheds. Ginger is the wizard where motorcycle engines are concerned, whilst his pal, Algie, is unmechanical but a mathematical genius. The two chums, the brightest specimens of the upper fifth, are looking forward to meeting the Major who had spent so much time in India and is keen to understand the meaning of 'horses' as applied to the record breaking home-made engine which the pair have so carefully constructed in a shed on the corner of his country estate. And so on...

Making the most of their holidays.

1930 – 1939

Schoolboys all looked like this in the thirties. Eric Bovey and George Rattery perched on the BSA were on their way home from school and paused for a while to admire the bike. and to ask the inevitable questions. What'll it do? How much was it? Can I have a go? What's that for? Actually the two boys look almost big enough to get a bike of their own. In the days when this picture was taken they would have just gone to the village school and left when they were aged fourteen to go to work. It would have been an uncertain time for them in the early thirties and at the height of the depression. Whether or not they had aspirations to go on to further education was often down to what their parents could afford, particularly if the boys' potential earning power outweighed any future considerations of higher academic aspirations. PHOTO HALSGROVE CHS

The Bournemouth to Swanage Motor Road & Ferry Company started their 400-yard steam-driven service across the entrance of Poole Harbour between Swanage and Poole in 1926. Despite its short season it proved very popular, and carried 100 000 passengers and 12 000 cars. Technically it is a floating bridge, being held in place and driven through chains attached to either bank. The fashion-conscious young lady is sitting on a 557cc side-valve Ariel from the mid thirties and looks as if she is all ready for a day on the beach, with her cushions strapped on the back. The operator has his hand on the engine-room telegraph ready to move the handle from stop to full ahead as the ferry takes up the slack on its chains. The lady has her camera case open and ready to take a picture, but the weather, judging by their clothing, doesn't look too promising.

Opposite top: Bill and Wentworth Harris ran a hardware shop in Anchor Street, Watchet. They were able to supply all the kind of things needed to keep a house running, and if necessary enough materials to build one. They also seemed to have specialised in weighing machines, proudly advertising the fact in their window. The Triumph sidecar outfit pulled up outside their shop was probably about ten or fifteen years old by the time this picture was taken in the nineteen thirties, it still has its old gas lights in place although they were rapidly becoming obsolete at the time. Triumph made and supplied their own sidecars, named the Gloria. Bill Harris, leaning against the wall chats to Violet Hill and her friend in the chair.   PHOTO HALSGROVE CHS

Opposite bottom: Peter Bradley was a Works' rider for Sunbeams specialising in sidecar work. This shot from the early thirties shows the team refuelling in one of the Trials that they entered, and quite often won. The picture shows the prevalent attitude to the dangers of fire; the scant regard paid to the petrol being poured from an open container which looks like a milk jug, via a funnel into the tank when there are at least two people in very close proximity who are smoking cigarettes. The sidecar passenger casually draws on his pipe and wonders how to keep his hands dry in those wet gloves, whilst simultaneously reading the route map and making sure the driver sticks to the regulations of the competition.

Above: Another shot of Peter Bradley doing routine maintenance on his Sunbeam outfit in 1930. The bike is probably a few years old at this stage, having a 'flat tank' rather than the recently introduced saddle tank. What is striking is the immaculate dress of Bradley. Not for him the greasy overalls and flat hat of the average mechanic. Sporting his immaculate white Oxford Bags trousers, sports jacket and old school tie he seems the most unlikely person to be an expert sidecar driver. It looks as though there has been some problem with the sidecar axle, and Bradley does have a trace of oily fingers, but still the smile is gleaming, the hair perfectly parted. There is not the slightest hint of panic or discomfort here; just get on with it despite the circumstances.

Opposite, top: Vyvyan Skidmore sits astride his Scott at Meavy on the South West slopes of Dartmoor in 1930. This mid twenties Flying Squirrel probably represented the marque at the height of its career. Subsequent efforts to keep up with the times brought elaboration and overweight that militated against its squirrel-like agility and its utter simplicity. The 498cc two-stroke engine was watercooled, and the oil was carried in a separate compartment in the distinctively shaped purple petrol tank. The radiator was mounted prominently in front of the engine and most owners kept the brass highly polished. This machine has carbide lights, but the generator for the gas is mounted by the rear fork, a long way from the lights for the gas to travel! Passengers on this particular Scott may have had an uncomfortable journey perched on the bicycle saddle fitted to the rear carrier. PHOTO HALSGROVE CHS

Opposite, bottom: The Reverend William Burgess of St Decumen's church in Watchet was able to get around his parish and to visit his congregation by using this little James. Known as the 'Pineapple' because of the unusual casting of the cylinder-barrel cooling fins, this machine was getting on a bit when the picture was taken in the thirties. The little belt-driven 225cc two stroke came from its Greet, Birmingham, factory around 1914. It is really quite dated; there are two gears, but it is belt-driven and still has the old carbide lights. Country parsons did not make huge amounts of money, and the impecunious vicar probably picked it up quite cheaply. Still, they were very reliable if looked after, and could carry a passenger, albeit at a funereal pace. The Bonniksen speedometer could well have been the most expensive item on the bike! PHOTO HALSGROVE CHS

From one world war to another, Art Deco was the very visual embodiment of the 1920s and 1930s. The graphics used in this catalogue illustration of a late thirties Matchless reflect a sense of time and place, the basic colours and stylised logo suggesting that not only can you buy a very good product, but that you will also be part of the very latest fashion when you go out on your 'Clubman'. Realistically the illustrator did choose to dress the rider in winter clothing rather than using the popular trick of finding the hottest summer day where minimal dress could be depicted.

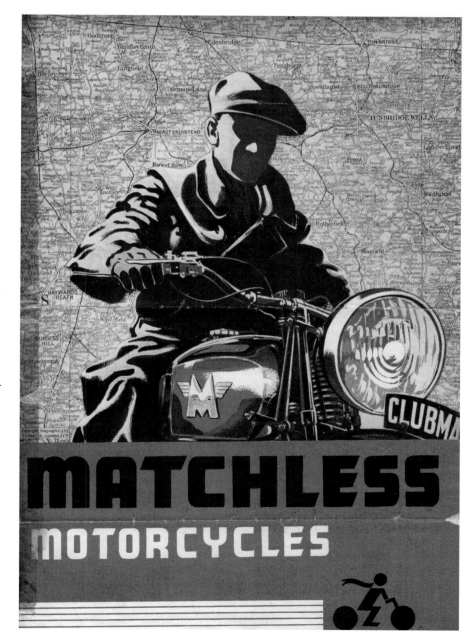

A lively group of young people have come down to the seaside for the weekend from the big city. They are camping and most have brought their bicycles, although they have not ridden all the way. In the late fifties you could get a train from Bristol to Barnstaple, and put the two-wheelers in the guard's van. Then it was only a short ride to Woolacombe and the campsite. A few of the wealthier have come down on a motorbike, forsaking the pleasures

of the crowded bank holiday special trains, preferring instead to risk breakdowns and traffic jams, but knowing that if they got there then they would have a lot less pushing to do than the others.

Opposite: Many people who bought motorcycles wanted to fix them at home, rather than take them to a dealer. Ex-servicemen had learned a lot of skills whilst in the forces, but they still needed detailed information on their own particular vehicles. A marketing opportunity arose when publishers realised that instruction books and manuals were needed to fill this gap, and from the mid twenties on these started to become available for the general public. Not just different makes were covered; there were hints and tips for motorcyclists, route maps, and a whole plethora of literature to back up the hobby and pastime of motorcycling.

Below: It's been raining hard, but the sun has come out just as they reached their destination. These two on their 1933 249cc model WA Triumph seem happy enough and well equipped to withstand anything the weather can throw at them. They both have oilskins and waders, she is carrying the rucksack and the map case, and he just sits up front. The bike is also partially enclosed against the elements, and in the fashion of that year it had an inclined engine and twin exhaust pipes issuing from its single cylinder engine.

PITMAN'S MOTOR CYCLISTS LIBRARY

The BOOK *of the* VILLIERS ENGINE

2⅙
NET

SIR ISAAC PITMAN & SONS LTD.

Cigarette cards were first introduced in the 1880s to stiffen the packages in which the cigarettes were sold, and subsequently as a way of advertising tobacco brands. Wills' and Ogden's were some of the leading producers of these cards for their cigarettes, but Brooke Bond also issued collectable cards in their packets of tea. They were printed in themes with usually between 25 and 50 in the set. Albums could be bought to display each collection, and this homeless little group of cards were used for 'swaps'. Mostly dating from the thirties, at least one of the motorcycles reflects the fashion for streamlining that has also been adopted by the 'Coronation Scot'.

The forecourt of Clark's Garage at Kessingland, Norfolk in the early thirties. The motorcycles include two almost brand new Scotts together with other unidentifiable bikes and cars. The petrol pumps are of some interest; the one on the left is a 'pot belly' from the early twenties, whilst the taller one is a 'Theo Multiple', made in Liverpool and designed to dispense six different brands of petrol which could be viewed in the glass window at the top of the pump. These were cheaper to install than a whole bank of pumps, and saved a lot of forecourt space.

Below: Brothers Cyril, Alf and Fred Bulpin were all keen motorcyclists, and had this picture taken of the three of them together at Sampford Brett, Crowcombe in Somerset, in 1931. It's interesting to see how, despite the machines being of differing makes, the boys have all got similar handlebar layouts. Their bulb horns are ready for action and their gas lights are polished and ready for the night ahead. The point about those gas lights was that they used a real flame to work, and the amount of light created depended on keeping the jets clean and at the same time having the correct focal length between the flame and the mirror in the back of the light. Dissolved calcium carbide in a special dispenser provided the gas, but keeping it alight at speed and in the wet was not always guaranteed if there was a leak. Carrying spare carbide was always a good thing, but providing water if you ran out could be tricky. There are many variations on the tales about how men meeting an unfortunate fellow rider on a darkened motorbike at night would fill the empty water reservoir in the way that only men can after a night out on the beer. Next day a letter would arrive thanking them for help, signed by a Miss so and so. This story is told so often that it actually assumes the status of an urban myth. PHOTO HALSGROVE CHS

Edgar Ward out in 1932 with Stenner's sidecar outfit delivering bread around Porlock. Commercial sidecars were available from many manufacturers; it made sense that if you could carry passengers then you could also carry goods. Often the shop owners only had the one vehicle, so for weekends they kept a spare passenger sidecar body and swapped it over as required. The front and side of the box represented a great opportunity for advertising and many showed off the signwriters art in all its glory. Most motorcycles by this stage were well up to the task of hauling quite heavy or bulky loads around; the advent of big engines combined with good gearboxes and clutches, reasonable stopping power and reliability made them a favourite means of tradesmen's transport; that is until, inevitably, the light van eventually took over these tasks. PHOTO HALSGROVE CHS

In the days before the Second World War, farmers were allowed to sell the milk from their cows straight to the milkman or to the public without having to bother with all the health and safety rules that apply nowadays. Most farmers, and people who worked on the land, were not averse to actually squirting milk straight from the cow's udder into their mouths in order to slake their thirst. Milk coolers had been invented; even so it was not uncommon for bottled milk to still be warm when it was delivered. The process of distribution was quite simple, the milkman rolled up on your doorstep with a big churn of milk, you supplied the bottle or whatever container you chose to keep your milk, then he would get a measure on a long handle and simply ladle it out from the churn; pints, quarts and even gallons. Jersey cows' milk was very good for cream, but Devonshires and Ayrshires provided quantity. You might buy some eggs, possibly the odd rabbit or pigeon as well. Just don't look too closely at the muck on the sides of the churn! Farmer Cyril Nichols has just supplied a full churn to milkman Bill Hooper at Mill Farm near Watchet in about 1930. PHOTO HALSGROVE CHS

The Parish of Shaugh stretches from the outskirts of Plymouth right up on to the more remote parts of Dartmoor. It is farming country, but also a place where china clay was mined in some quantity. Frank and Winifred Lillicrap, here shown in 1931, would have been able to make the journey into the centre of Plymouth on their BSA in an hour or less. Plymouth was a huge naval town, its dockyards buzzing with activity, and the town centre itself alive with shops, pubs, theatres and so on. To dress up in your finest clothes was the normal thing to do on a Saturday outing, and Frank and Winifred certainly look very smart. The problem then, as now, was what to wear if it rains or you don't want to get cold. Perhaps this is really a posing shot, and tucked away out of sight are oilskins and sou'westers which were for proper motorcycle journeys. PHOTO HALSGROVE CHS

Commercial sidecars were used by all kinds of public utility companies in the thirties. Here, Geoffrey Norman, a maintenance plumber for the Watchet Water Company, cautiously guides his outfit along the narrow Gladstone Terrace. The sidecar appears to be a home-made box, perfectly suited to carrying tools, lengths of water pipe, ladders and whatever the jobbing plumber might need to carry on his trade. There are no lights on the bike, so daytime only then; no emergency call outs in the middle of the night! PHOTO HALSGROVE CHS

Looking for all the world like James Cagney in one of his gangster films, George Chidgey sits on his 499cc Rudge Special, whilst his pillion passenger, Ted Stevens, pats his shoulder reassuringly. Taken in Williton in the mid thirties the Speediron was one of the machines made by the Rudge Whitworth Company in Coventry. Interestingly the firm had run into financial difficulties despite their racing successes and the sale of proprietary engines and gearboxes which they sold under the name of 'Python'. The company was taken over in 1934 by EMI, of gramophone fame, and production was moved to Hayes in Middlesex a few years later. However when the war started, EMI devoted all its efforts to building radar equipment so motorcycle manufacture ended. EMI sold Rudge Whitworth interests to Sturmey Archer and Norman Motorcycles, and they in turn passed it on to Raleigh in 1943. PHOTO HALSGROVE CHS

Opposite, top: Another one of those 'see how many we can get on a motorbike' photographs. These ladies from Cullompton in 1932 are enthusiastic about the game, although there are only three seated, far short of a record! Mother, standing in the doorway looks on indulgently, girls will be girls! The bike is not readily identifiable, possibly a BSA. PHOTO HALSGROVE CHS

Opposite, bottom: What more typically English scene could you imagine? It's a hot summer's day in the mid thirties, and Wrythe Green near Carshalton basks in the midday heat. The name Wrythe is derived from the Anglo Saxon rithe, meaning stream or possibly it came from the rye which was once grown in the fields around here. The small boys with their home-made cart rest in the shade of the tree; the green is perfectly manicured and roped off. In the street at the back there is a rag and bone man with his hand cart. The motorcycle and sidecar is able to park wherever it pleases, there being little other traffic around. However this is not the rural idyll it may at first appear, according to the signpost, it is only 10 miles to London. PHOTO HALSGROVE CHS

Above: The little AJS and its rider in his best blazer are just off on a short holiday. The photograph was taken in the early part of 1940, so the young man would be due for imminent call up, but for the moment he can forget the war and just enjoy riding in the almost deserted Worcestershire countryside around Leigh and Bransford. A J Stevens was an old established firm who made a range of single- and twin-cylinder motorcycles, and had a huge string of racing successes with their Big Port and Overhead Camshaft models. By the time this 1932 250cc was made, the firm had been taken over by the Matchless concern, yet the AJS name continued well into the sixties as a separate entity. PHOTO HALSGROVE CHS

Opposite: Rudge had a reputation for producing well made but pricey machines, and by 1938 the market was difficult, so sales continued to be depressed. The radial four-valve engine had been given valve enclosure to bring it right up to date and remained a fixture at the core of the Rudge range of motorcycles until production ended in 1940. The first Rudge to be given the name 'Ulster' celebrated the firm's success in the 1928 Ulster Grand Prix, their 'Special' was a slightly detuned version of the 499cc model. At Truro just before the war started, and in the shadow of Brunel's viaduct which crosses the city just beyond the railway station, a local fireman who is the proud owner of a brand new 'Special' admires his purchase. PHOTO HALSGROVE CHS

Right: As the depression of the early thirties ebbed, BSA began to offer machines which were a little more than just basic transport. They revised their 350cc and 500cc engines, put them into up-to-date cycle parts and named the range 'Blue Stars'. Reg Derham is seated on one of the last of the range, a 1936 499cc model, at West Huntspill. The chrome-plated upswept exhaust pipes and stylish tank made this a most admired motorcycle, the electric lighting kit, previously an optional extra had been fitted as standard a few years before. In late 1936 this bike had an entirely different engine designed by Val Page and became the Empire Star, and it was one of these with an all alloy, bench-tested engine that BSA gained a Brooklands Gold Star in the hands of Wal Handley. It inspired the factory to launch another new model, named after its Brooklands success, the 'Gold Star'. PHOTO HALSGROVE CHS

Bill Carpenter Senior with sons Walter, Percy and Bill junior off to a football match in Silverton north of Exeter in 1933. Of all the contenders for the 'how many on a motorbike' competition (Dad is on a push bike behind the brothers), these three look as if they might actually be going somewhere. In fact if it's winter and they are about to play a game then the pitch can't be far away otherwise, dressed like this, they would just get too cold to function either on or off the field. The *Daily Gazette* doesn't mention their match on its billboard, but there has been a disastrous fire on a farm close by that might deserve their attention. The bike is a mid twenties Sunbeam Lion. PHOTO HALSGROVE CHS

Above: The Higginson's domestic staff, at Stinsford House near Dorchester, take a break on the front doorstep in May 1935. Stinsford House is a Grade II listed building which stands next to the church where Thomas Hardy's heart is buried. It was once one of two great estates which dominated the parish of Stinsford and which Hardy called Mellstock in *Under the Greenwood Tree*. The house, like so many others, eventually became dilapidated and was sold on. In later years it was renovated and turned into a boarding school. The Ariel belonging to Mr Higginson is a 'Sloper' 350cc MF, introduced in 1931.   PHOTO HALSGROVE CHS

Below: Count how many there are on this bike. It's taken in India, and shows a group of Colonial Officers and their friends having a bit of fun on the lawns of the British Embassy. The bike is a mid thirties OK Supreme with a JAP engine, but it has been somewhat modified by the removal of the front mudguard and headlight, suggesting that perhaps in its past life it had had a front-end collision. The influence of the British opened up all kinds of markets to motorcycle manufacturers and in turn the factories exported as many of their machines as they could.

Above: The American four-cylinder Henderson was one of the superbikes of the twenties and early thirties. By 1930 the 1305cc engine could get the bike up to 100mph, although in the following year the Detroit factory making the machines closed for business finally and quite unexpectedly. This particular example is a 1930 Streamline which was noted for the graceful lines of its 'fenders' and tank. They were very popular with the police who used them extensively in the United States. Ding Dong is in area of old tin mines near Land's End in Cornwall. It was closed in 1879 although a few later attempts were made to restart operations, but these failed fairly quickly. The name of this mine has nothing to do with the nursery rhyme, there are songs written about the place, and a bell in Madron was rung as the last shift of workers came off duty.

Opposite, top: Brooklands, to the south of London, was the place to be seen before the war if you were at all interested in speed. The closeness of spectators to the racing, the smell of the castor oil and the roar of the engines were all very much part of the enjoyment. Often only a wicker fence separated the paying public from competitors, and this hallowed piece of British concrete was the scene of many dramatic performances. Spectators are a little thin on the ground in this mid week race, as the Matchless outfit ridden by P Brackpool, leads the pack. It is interesting to note how standard these combinations are, definitely motorcycles with sidecars unlike modern racing outfits which are built with a single monocoque chassis; there being no way that the bike could be ridden as a solo.

Opposite, bottom: Plenty of hand holds are needed to accommodate the gymnastics performed by this sidecar passenger on a Matchless and Wasonian at a 1931 meeting at Layham's Farm, West Wickham, Kent. The outfit is owned and ridden by members of the Brackpool family who ran it partly to publicise their South East London business. They were Matchless agents, and knew the Collier Brothers, owners of Matchless, very well. Their shop was not far from the Matchless factory and their bikes were semi-Works sponsored, with specially modified bits and pieces going into the engines and frames. On occasions, the Colliers entered races using pre-production prototypes which were undergoing the kind of rigorous testing that only hard competition like grass tracking could provide.

In 1933 Germany was the third-best foreign customer for British factories. However these were not all complete machines as quite a number of the German factories were fitting JAP or Sturmey Archer engines, Druid forks, and other British-made accessories. By 1934 this had changed, with severe duties having to be paid on imports from Britain. The rise of the German industry in the thirties and its attempts to become pre eminent in the competition field only recently dominated by the British is exemplified by these three DKW riders. DKW had pioneered the concept of the split single. It is reputed that the 1938 supercharged version could be heard in Liverpool whilst going down Bray Hill in the Isle of Man. The riders are wearing the Nazi insignia on their leathers, just to reinforce their identity.

Once you could just about ride wherever you wanted. There were few restrictions, most people didn't seem to mind if you were inclined to take your bike off the tarred road and on to the kind of tracks that had been the norm only forty or so years before. This little girder-forked, rigid-framed James would have been OK in the dry and dust, but on the chalk the skinny tyres would have found little in the way of grip. This photo, if taken nowadays and not in the nineteen thirties, would show two very wide parallel sets of tyre tracks, but in this picture there is a central track where horses walked and two narrower ruts where the cartwheels would have gone.

The sheltered sides of the Tamar Valley have for many years been a place where small horticultural farms have grown fruit and vegetables, principally to supply the nearby markets of Plymouth, South Devon, and by using the railways even as far away as London and the Midlands. The steepness of the ground made the early use of machinery difficult, but an enterprising and inventive owner adapted an old Raleigh motorcycle into a winch. The idea was that with the engine started and the machine manoeuvred into position and firmly lashed to a tree at the top of the sloping field, a long wire rope could be paid out by using the guides and rollers. This in turn was attached to a small hoe or plough, and hauled uphill doing the work that may once have been done by a horse. At the top the operator would move the winch on a bit, pull the plough back down to the bottom and start all over again.

Motorcycle Clubs would regularly hold open days where they could show off their bikes, recruit new members and hold what were known as gymkhanas. These were, as the name suggests, loosely based on horse events, and provided an opportunity for members to entertain with their riding skills, and also to have some fun in a rather more relaxed manner than might otherwise be the case. Here, in the early fifties, members of Pendennis Motorcycle Club in Falmouth use their old BSAs to do some trick riding for the benefit of the crowd. There seemed to be few issues here regarding health and safety issues, what with no helmets and young children riding high up on the passenger's shoulders. PHOTO FRAN PARKER

Around the mid thirties Phil Vincent became disillusioned with fitting 'bought in' engines to his HRD machines. He decided that he would build one of his own, and supposedly came up with this design in just four months. He had already built his Meteor engine, but this version was a lightly-tuned version of it and he called it a 'Comet'. It had rear suspension and a high camshaft 499cc specification. In itself it was extremely successful and continued in production until the mid fifties. When Phil Vincent doubled it up and made a V-twin out of it, a legend was created. This Cornish-registered Comet, photographed near St Day, was owned by Mr Chard and used as a ride-to-work bike.

PHOTO FRAN PARKER

Below: The Levis factory, probably due as much as anything to their competition successes had a worldwide following. They exported many machines, to Australia for instance, and here is a line up of around twenty-five machines that were presented as part of the Victoria Motorcycle Week in Melbourne; the date was 25 September 1937. The Birmingham factory produced motorcycles in their factory up to the beginning of the Second World War. Visible in this line up are mostly overhead valve four-strokes, with capacities of 350, 498 and 600cc. British manufactured machines were very popular in both Australia and New Zealand, and there remain many examples left in that part of the world from the time when British was best. PHOTO J VICKERS

Betty Payne sits on her future husband's Ariel outside her home near Dorchester. Following the depression years of the 1930s Ariel ran into financial difficulties, but Jack Sangster whose family had been involved with the company since Victorian times managed to save it. His range of single-cylinder Red Hunter machines in 248cc, 346cc and 499cc versions became known for their toughness and reliability for many years to come. In fact the last of the Red Hunters, direct descendants of this particular machine came off the production line in 1959. Betty Payne would go on to marry Dennis Jenkins the owner of this mid thirties single.

PHOTO HALSGROVE CHS

Below: The 21st International Six Days' Trial started on 31 August 1939 in Germany. Teams from Britain were getting little in the way of up-to-date news, although they knew there was growing tension between Germany and many of the other countries whose riders had entered the Trial. By the fifth day, Friday, Major Watling of the ACU and Peter Bradley the former Sunbeam Works' rider who was manager of the British Team, decided to pull out and try to get everyone to Switzerland. The situation was grave, but petrol was arranged and Obergruppenfuhrer Kraus, the president of the jury controlling the Trial, stated that he would escort all visiting riders to the frontier to make sure there were no incidents. All went well, and every member of the British team was eventually able to get back home safely. The photograph shows Major Watling and Peter Bradley discussing the latest news at the beginning of that fateful week.

The dispatch rider was a very important member of the Armed Forces during the Second World War. This rider on his 500cc side-valve 16h Norton is studying a map which he has contrived to wind around the tube mounted on his bars. The standard issue map case which dangled from the DR's neck would usually fly around behind, or get wet and twisted up, so he had to stop and spend what seemed like hours sorting it out in order to read the route. The photograph was taken 'somewhere in England' on an exercise leading up to D-Day, in this case escorting medical trucks. Dispatch riders' duties included not only the collecting and deliveries of signals, but also the escort of convoys and general policing of traffic on the routes. The cigarette aids concentration; the rider look as though he has been up all night; this was arduous work, especially in the blackout.

The photograph depicts a scene of utter devastation on the beach at Dunkirk after the evacuation of British Troops had been completed. The motorcycle had done its very best, it just could not take its rider any further. The order would have been to destroy all vehicles to stop them falling into enemy hands. There were many drivers and riders who found it very difficult to do this job as they had grown very fond of their own particular transport, and it felt like getting rid of an old friend. Nevertheless, orders were orders. The sump plugs were taken out so that the oil drained away into the sand. Engines were started and revved until they grew red hot and finally seized solid, and then they were left as scrap.

Below: This German Army propaganda photograph shows a dump of captured British motorcycles left behind at Dunkirk. The sidecar outfit is a Norton Big 4, fitted with sidecar wheel drive. The BSA and Matchless lying on their side include what seems to be an impressed model, which is a civilian specification version of the 350 ohv, and showing its unmilitary origins by having a panel in the tank. The bikes have been sorted and stacked in an orderly fashion, as have the pile of lorry chassis in the background. The national eagle and swastika badges on the tunics and jackboots leave no room for doubt that these German troops are in charge of the situation.

Private Royce Stoneman of the 6th Battalion the Devonshire Regiment at North Tawton. Young Royce is seen here in his army uniform after being called up to fight in the county regiment. This is not any Army motorcycle; it's a civilian BSA from the mid thirties, identified by the hand gear change and the AA badge, although it does have a blackout mask on the headlight. The blackout masks were designed to make any vehicle's progress invisible to enemy aircraft, thus keeping important positions hidden from the fliers. To drive during the hours of darkness, especially in the blackout, was most difficult. Vehicles of the time had at best pretty poor lights compared with modern standards anyway. The meagre 6-volt glow was greatly reduced by the louvers on the mask, and as a result there were many wartime accidents. The rear lights were likewise shielded and it was very hard to see any vehicles, even big trucks, if you came up behind them. PHOTO HALSGROVE CHS

Below: Parting is such sweet sorrow, especially when you have to say goodbye to your motorbike and go off to war. Here Bob Meatyard and his mates are taking leave of their home and family in Richmond Place, Wincanton. The young man with the glasses looks as if he has half wings on the sleeve of his RAF battledress; this means that he was probably aircrew rather than the actual pilot of an aircraft. It emphasises just how young some of the combatants were. It was often the case, for instance, that a teenager could pilot an aircraft into action against the enemy, yet not have passed his driving test back in Britain. The 'L' plates on the bike suggest that at least one of the young people pictured here did not have too much experience on two wheels. PHOTO HALSGROVE CHS

The Army had a task system for everyday regular maintenance on all their vehicles, from tanks to motorcycles, ambulances to machine gun carriers; check the oil, the bearings, coolant, fuel and so on. In this way any major breakdowns might be avoided. But of course when you are a dispatch rider you have to be able to fix your own bike in an emergency, especially when you are far from the base workshops. Whilst his mates look on and pour themselves another cup of tea, this DR has the primary chaincase off his BSA M20, and is adjusting the clutch with his own spanners from the toolkit that he carries with him. Perhaps there is something else troubling him, you don't normally take the tank off to do the clutch, unless perhaps a cable has broken.

This DR sweating in the hot sun is having real gearbox problems with his BSA. There are a couple of spare boxes out on the floor, so this was probably taken at a proper workshop. The gear change lever is on the ground, so maybe there was a problem with one of the selectors. The BSA M20 was a 500cc side-valve machine that was well over-engineered, although it was slow and had little ground clearance. However it would take a lot of abuse, especially from the not particularly mechanically-minded squaddies that had to ride it in conditions that ranged from the deserts of North Africa to the cold winter snows of Holland and Belgium.

Some parts of Britain in the early 1940s were barely touched by the war that was going on. The remote farms and villages carried on with their old way of life pretty much as before, unaffected by bombing raids or military manoeuvres. There was often plenty to eat; farm and garden produce being readily available, although shortages of petrol and other commodities did make inroads into the cost of living. There were evacuees to be billeted and the Ministry of Agriculture made its presence felt. Still, these two young ladies at Blackabrook Farm on Dartmoor seem to be enjoying themselves. Marge is sitting on the Ariel, whilst 'Cheel' is aboard the Sunbeam. 'Cheel' is a dialect word for a little girl. PHOTO HALSGROVE CHS

One of the more desirable machines that the War Department ordered was this Matchless G3L. Earlier versions had girder forks, as shown in this head-on shot taken in 1941, but by the middle of the war the factory had developed the teledraulic front fork. This telescopic device gave a much smoother ride than the older system, and combined with the lively performance from its 350 ohv engine, made it one of the most sought after bikes to ride. Probably the next most desirable DR bike was the Ariel W/NG, another lively 350, and thereafter there were the normal BSA, Norton and Royal Enfield's which most people seem to have had some experience of. This factory photograph shows the Matchless when it was new, in use it would probably have lost the tyre pump, horn and its pristine paint job. It was Army practice that if a respray was necessary, then the machine would be stood up against a wall and the whole lot painted, saddle and all; after all there was a war on!

Ernest 'Doc' Northam was a young Cornish dispatch rider serving with the RASC in Italy in 1943. He had come by way of Palestine, and the deserts of North Africa where he had fought alongside the 7th Armoured Division. Later, he was ferried across the Mediterranean to Italy, and still riding his much loved Matchless started to work his way up towards the Volturno River. One day he rode up behind a slow moving convoy and was given the go ahead to pass, but part way through the manoeuvre a lorry appeared coming towards him. There was nowhere to go, and as a result of the inevitable crash Doc Northam died of his injuries. He is buried in the Military cemetery in Assisi. PHOTO A NORTHAM

The war in the North African desert was a mobile one, where transport, fuel and the ability to maintain vehicles were paramount in importance. Here, Peter Miles on his BSA M20 adopts the normal casual DR wear and sets off for Tac HQ with a message. The M20 ran hot at the best of times, and in the blazing desert conditions there were times when the exhaust pipe glowed red. Awkward and heavy it may have been, but the BSA was massively over-engineered and proved very reliable and easily maintained by the people who had to ride them. The black out mask was an adornment that was required on all types of transport, but perhaps not so necessary in the desert where most vehicle movements happened during daylight hours.

Petrol rationing meant that many motorcycles had to be taken off the road during the war, or perhaps the big bikes were put away and smaller mopeds were brought out instead. Petrol coupons were available for special war work however, and this mid thirties Triumph 6/1 600cc side-valve sidecar outfit, wearing its regulation blackout mask, was used by an engineer to get to his essential war work in an aircraft factory. He did use it occasionally at weekends however, and the two girls seem to be having a nice day out as a result. It was not unknown for certain aircrew and ground staff to use aircraft fuel in their own vehicles, although if you were caught doing this then the penalties could be quite extreme.

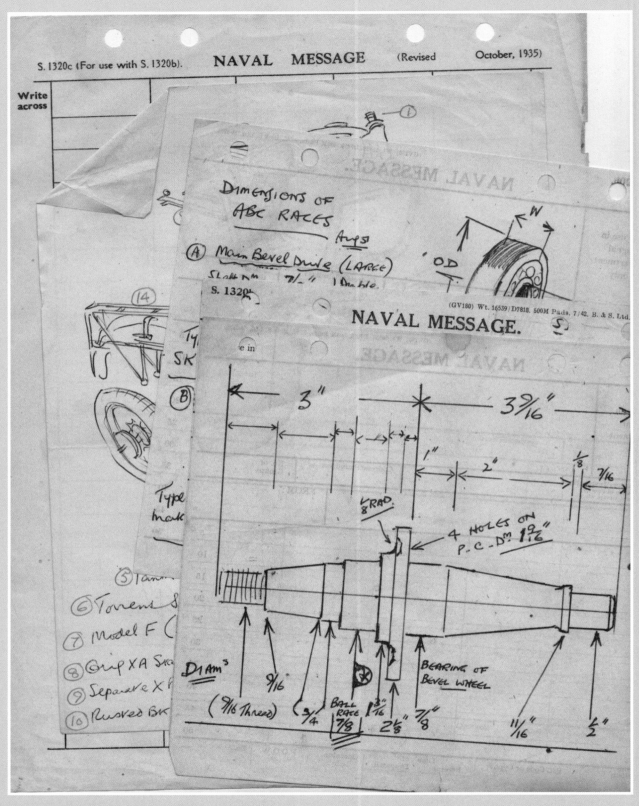

Too old to fight in the war, George Heywood of Plymouth worked in the dockyards as a clerk, sending and receiving messages and generally doing what clerks do. Between moments of frantic activity, there were long and boring periods when George's thoughts turned to his beloved ABC and Douglas motorcycles. Not only was he a talented engineer, he was also a good artist, and these doodles are the result. He lovingly recorded all kinds of information and technical details of his restoration jobs on the paper which came most readily to hand. And of course with the engineering resources that could keep a modern warship afloat, George had access to certain areas of expertise which, had he worked elsewhere, he might not have been able to benefit from.

Longleys   'NORTON MOTORS LTD., BIRMINGHAM

During the Second World War sidecar outfits played a less important role than they had in the Great War. Still, Norton made an outfit based on its 600cc Big Four which saw service. The sidecar wheel was driven by a shaft attached to the rear wheel, although there was no differential. This meant that the Norton was very difficult to steer on firm surfaces; it had a tendency to go in a straight line. Off road it was fine, and many were sent to France before Dunkirk, but inevitably nearly all had to be abandoned. There was also a batch used quite successfully in the North African desert, where the sand was much more forgiving to the two driven wheels. When the Jeep arrived it spelt the end of the fighting sidecar outfit in Allied hands, although the Germans continued to use them right up to the end of the European war.

The American Harley Davidson Company built 88 000 of their 750 twins for the war effort. It was called the WLA, (the A stood for American, while WLCs were Canadian) and it had a very low compression, enlarged cylinder head finning, and a big air cleaner. There was a huge bash plate under the crankcase and it could carry lots of luggage including a rifle. It was no great performer, just about managing 50mph with all that equipment on board, yet it gained a reputation for absolute reliability which endeared it to thousands of GIs. After the war, those that remained in the UK were bought up, civilianised and sold on to an eager market of recently demobbed servicemen. Possibly the young man pictured here on his Canadian WLC version had just spent his wartime gratuity on it, whatever he seems very pleased with his new purchase.

Indian's response to the war was blighted by the run-down condition of its factory, and they failed to capture the lion's share of the military orders. They built a version of their well-known Scout designated the 640. Reputedly a ship load of these machines was torpedoed in the Atlantic and so there are a lot less of them around than the rival Harleys. This bike is still pretty much in the condition that it left the army, with much of its military equipment present. Wellies seem a trifle incongruous here!

Here Alf Brown sits aboard his James outside Ivy Cottage in Princetown on Dartmoor. The year is 1947 and Alf, wearing his demob suit, looks pretty pleased with his new transport. The James' lightweights were developed from the military models which had been supplied to the armed forces during World War 2. Although the factory had been badly damaged by German bombs in 1940, still over 6000 machines were produced for the war effort. The little 122cc Villiers engine could propel the bike along at speeds that might reach 40 mph. As a basic means of getting about it wasn't bad, and the cost of £53 6s 10d ultimately made it a good deal. PHOTO HALSGROVE CHS

In 1945 Leslie Lingwood was finally released from a Prisoner of War camp in Germany and was able to return to his home at Sculthorpe near Fakenham in Norfolk. To celebrate, Leslie could take his bike for a ride once again, and give it a good thrashing over the flat fenland roads of the surrounding area. The bike itself is quite interesting. It looks like one of the very rare Ariel 500cc side-valve machines that were produced for a short period at the beginning of the war. Ariel's main military model was the well-regarded 350cc ohv W/NG but this is a W/VA and is quite different to the 350. Its main use was as a second-line defence machine; some were equipped with sidecars. Small quantities were supplied to the Air Ministry and the Ministry of Agriculture notably for use by the Womens Land Army. The machine which Leslie Lingwood is riding may well have been civilianised with new paint, although its military origins are given away by the sight of the field stand poking out beside the rear fork.
PHOTO HALSGROVE CHS

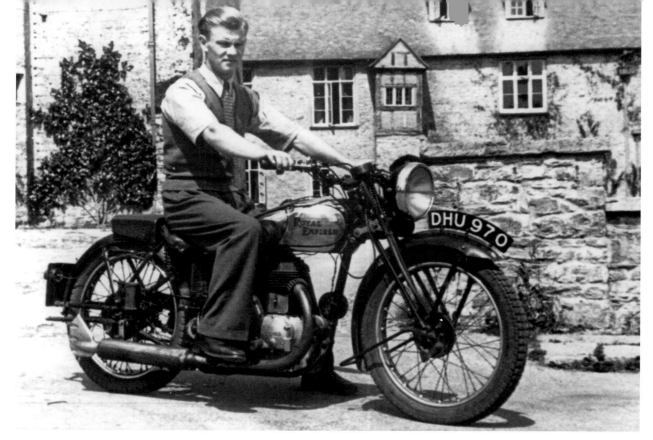

Ted King of Dartington is seen here on his girder-forked Royal Enfield in the late 1940s. During the Second World War Enfield made around 55 000 dispatch riders' machines. Besides the side-valve and overhead valve models there was the 'Flying Flea' designed to be collapsible for use by paratroops and other airborne forces. After the war, Enfield bought back many of the machines it had made for the war effort, painted them black, and then sold them on to the public. PHOTO HALSGROVE CHS

Below: In the years immediately following the war, both AJS and Matchless capitalised on the popularity of their wartime models. In effect the only real difference between the two 350cc models was the position of the magneto; Matchless to the rear of the cylinder, AJS at the front. Tony Pigram is seen here riding his brother John's AJS, though his feet are barely touching the ground and he looks a bit young for a full riding license. PHOTO HALSGROVE CHS

There's something about crossroads and meetings. The annals of popular music are filled with anecdotes about people who met the devil there and in return for some gift he was able to bestow, they would sell him their soul. The great blues player Robert Johnson is said to have achieved fame and fortune in this way. Crossroads are also just a good place to meet, perhaps a lovers' tryst, or more mundanely to pick up some sandwiches from your mum on the way to work. Whatever the story, this meeting between the Ariel rider/photographer and the lady with the bicycle took place just after the war in rural Derbyshire. The Ariel is one of the newly revamped post-war 350cc NG models with a chrome tank filled with all kinds of glittery bits of oil gauge, clock, petrol cap, inspection light and so on. The ex WD panniers have been repainted to suit the rest of the bike.

Below: After the Second World War tourism and trade were beginning to make the main roads into Cornwall a lot busier than they had ever been. A really good location for a petrol station and garage business was therefore on the main spine road, the A30, into the county. Osborne & Sharpe had their garage in the village of Fraddon, and sold the usual petrol, tyres, oil and other car and motorcycle-related sundries. They were agents for Morris; there is a Morris Eight in the window, and alongside it there is a girder-forked Norton with a price card on it. This particular garage favoured PYE records and wireless sets for their customers. Osbornes were also haulage contractors, doing a lot of work for the nearby China Clay industry, hauling clay to the local ports for onward shipping to the rest of the UK and into Europe.

This painting, dated September 1946 and executed by someone called H Fiedler is of a nameless rider on a New Imperial, going for broke in a grass track meeting. This is an oil painting on canvas and properly mounted in a wooden frame. There is a certain amount of detective work that might usefully be done here. The leather helmet seems to be the kind of thing worn by German tank crews, the name Fiedler and the date may therefore indicate German origins. The New Imperial model 60 of 1939, a 346cc ohv model, as depicted here was listed as 'The Grand Prix'. The late thirties New Imps were based on their successful Works replicas, but by 1940 the firm had been sold to Triumph, and eventually just faded away, the name was not revived after the war. So perhaps this painting was done by a German POW, someone who was still in captivity, but who used his skills as an artist to turn photographs of British riders into works of art in exchange for money or goods that normally they would not have access to.

Landkey, a small village in North Devon, possessed a shop which could supply you with many everyday items, and beside it was a petrol station. There is no garage apparent in this photograph, so it was just a place you could go to fill up with whichever brand of fuel best suited your particular vehicle. On offer are products from Shell, Essolene and National Benzole. Price of premium grade petrol, as marked on the central pump is 1/7d a gallon. This dates the photograph to the immediate post Second World War years, when after rationing there still existed an agreement between the competing petrol companies that they should all sell their fuel at roughly the same price. The globes on top of the pumps were used to advertise the products, and if you look closely you can spot the handles which were used to crank the petrol out of the pumps by hand, there being no built in electric motors to do the job.
PHOTO HALSGROVE CHS

'That's my sister on there, she's eighty odd now, so you work out when it was taken. I swapped the cammy Velo for a little C12 BSA I had, mind you my bike was on the road and the chap just wanted something to get to work on. The Velo was in a bit of state, late twenties it was and not worth much at the time. It was hand change but converted to foot change. See the little bobby dodger flashlight on it, you could do that in those days. I spent quite a lot of time on it and got it running quite well. In the end I got rid of it and bought a Triumph instead, bit more reliable it was. Wish I had it now though!' Les Willis of St Austell talking about one of the bikes he owned in Somerset when he was young.

Below: The Motor Car Act of 1903 required all vehicles to be placed on a register and to carry number plates. In the case of motorcycles they needed a rear plate together with a double sided curved plate to fit on top of the front mudguard. The front number plate continued to be used right up until 1975 when it was discontinued because of the severe danger it represented to pedestrians in the event of an accident. When dealers put a new machine in their showroom they were issued with one of these special plates by the manufacturer for information purposes. The little Panther described here was rather underpowered, and its immediate ancestors had been built for Pride & Clark as a budget machine. Dismissed by many riders as 'Grey Porridge' the Panther nevertheless had its fair share of supporters.

Melville Mitchell of Bugle near St Austell is posing with his just post war Vincent-HRD Rapide on the harbour side at Looe. This was an entirely new post war model and created a lot of interest in motorcycle circles. The cost of this one in 1947 was £293.7s.5d, with the speedometer being £4 extra and the purchase tax £1 1s 8d. That was a lot of money back then! A test that was carried out on the bike did not get a top speed, but in third it managed 98mph! The ex RAF flying jacket and beret could not have afforded too much weather protection for the rider, but that probably counted for little under the circumstances. Incidentally, Martin's Dairy is still there, and anyone can park outside and get a delicious Cornish ice cream. PHOTO C EDYVEAN

Opposite: The young rider seated on this racing KTT Velocette is Barry Johnson, who later went on to have a long career with Amal carburettors. Barry started riding competitively soon after the war, and when he stopped racing he continued in the motorcycle industry. In the course of his work Barry attended many races, he was the 'Amal Man' at the Isle of Man TT races for instance, and helped advise on many record-breaking attempts by British factories and their products. He was the person called upon to design, in somewhat of a hurry, a carburettor suitable for replacing the monobloc and bringing the available range more up to date. Barry came up with the 'concentric', and this slimmer and more efficient instrument is still in use on many bikes today. PHOTO B JOHNSON

1950 – 1959

This Sunbeam belongs to Terence Baker of 44 West Street, East Coker near Yeovil. Although the scene is set in the 1950s, the bike is a pre war version of the Sunbeam Series 2, 350cc Sports model. Sunbeam had a great reputation for their build quality, and in particular for their paint finish. For a while they were owned by ICI, who supposedly were after the paint secrets and patents, but just before the war the company was sold to the AJS and Matchless combine in London because they weren't making the profits required of them. There were often two versions of the Sunbeam models, that is a road going one, and, as here, a sports version with high level exhaust. The price new was £66 and the top speed was 75mph.
PHOTO HALSGROVE CHS

This happy little band is outside the old Post Office at Willand. The date is 1952, and the scooter belongs to Charlie Copp. It is a Corgi, manufactured by the Brockhouse Engineering Company of Southport, and is a development of the war time Wellbike. It was very basic and proved popular for getting to work or shopping if it wasn't too far! It was available with a kick start, windshield and an enclosed body. Production ceased in 1954. Behind Charlie, a proud dad shows off his little girl who, dressed in her best summer frock, sits on the saddle of a rigid framed BSA twin, probably an A7 of the late forties. The big mystery is why the gentleman in the middle is holding a box of 'Tide' washing powder, which he had got in a half price sale, on his head!
PHOTO HALSGROVE CHS

It was the bike that everyone was supposed to have learned to ride on, or at least owned at some point in their riding careers. BSA's Bantam came off the production line just after the Second World War and was an immediate best seller. The design was based on the pre war German DKW, and was one of the most copied ever seen, there being home grown versions produced in the USA, Poland, East and West Germany, Japan and India. Ginger White of Lamerton bought this 125cc two stroke D1 in 1948; it was not called a 'Bantam' until a few months after its launch. The price of £76 4s 0d compared favourably with similar machines on offer at the time; bikes like a Royal Enfield Flying Flea, A James 122cc, or a Francis Barnett Merlin. The little BSA looks as if its already having a bit of a hard life, Ginger doesn't seem too worried about riding in his dirty boots and there's not exactly a pristine finish remaining at the time the picture was taken. PHOTO HALSGROVE CHS

Above: The temptation to get an old bike and see how it would go is exemplified by this shot of Mr A. Morley on his Ariel at a North Devon Motor Club's 'Novices and Observers Trial' held at Hartnoll Barton, Muddiford in March 1952. It looks as though Mr Morley has bought an ex army 350cc bike and modernised it with telescopic forks,

discarding the old fashioned girder forks it had when new. The bike has had some previous use off road, as evidenced by the battered and dented exhaust pipe. With no helmet or gloves and wearing a sports jacket and wellies, a serious Mr Morley 'gives it stick' up a slope to the approval of the spectators. You could buy much better bikes to do this on, but it was just fun on an old banger, and if you beat your mate so much the better!
PHOTO HALSGROVE CHS

Left: The LE (little engine) Velocette was a real break from Velocette's range of single-cylinder four-stroke machines. The water-cooled flat twin was aimed at the post war mass market, and it incorporated a host of new ideas which were supposed to appeal to all sectors of the population in their quest to find personalised transport. The little 150cc engine soon had another 50cc added to it, yet it never achieved the success that was hoped for it. It missed the scooter market, being still very much a motorcycle, but was too revolutionary for dyed-in-the-wool motorcyclists. The police used them extensively, after which they became known as 'Noddy Bikes'. This lady has chosen an ordinary raincoat to go out on her LE; with its hand-cranked starter and hand gear change the Velocette had many design similarities to the two-wheeled car that it emulated.

Victoria Garage near Roche on the old A30 not far from Bodmin was not just a place to fill up with petrol in the early fifties; you could also buy a cup of tea and a bacon sandwich there. This outing by members of Pendennis Motorcycle Club took place in heavy rain, and it's interesting to see how the riders equipped themselves for the bad weather. Certainly the local shops supplying ex War Department clothes had done very well. Visible are people wearing dispatch riders' coats, helmets and gauntlets, whilst others have chosen tank suits, flying helmets and RAF goggles. Most wear gumboots to keep their feet dry, whilst hobnailed army boots have not been left out. It didn't seem to matter too much about smoking in the area of the pumps either. PHOTO FRAN PARKER

What do you do when your son says he wants to get a bike just like his Dad? Different people react in different ways, not always positively. Here however we have a photo of a father and son who are approaching the subject positively. First get a new bike; perhaps a newly introduced 1953 150cc Triumph Terrier, the predecessor to the Cub. Then get decent clothing, like warm flying jackets and a pudding basin or corker helmet. The next thing is to go for the first ride, with Dad on the back to provide assistance and guidance. The bike was marketed as a commuter

bike which was also ideal for learners. Triumph hoped that if you got hooked into the brand early enough, then perhaps later you would go on to buy one of the bigger twins for which they were so famous. The looks are solemn; perhaps this is the first ride. It's not easy at the best of times to carry a pillion, especially if it's your Dad and he tries to steer from the back. Hopefully there was a positive result, and the test was passed.

Touring holidays on a motorcycle combination became very popular in the fifties, when people had money to spend and the desire to expand their horizons. The magazines printed all kinds of articles extolling the virtues of touring, including the crossing of the English Channel. One such article suggested that there were three kinds of motorcycle foreign tourists. There are those with high powered machines who put up prodigious mileages during a fortnight's holiday. Then there are those with a specific destination in mind who wished to get there as soon as possible and return to the same bed every night. The third group, possibly one to which this motorcyclist belongs, make a circular tour, staying a night or two here and there, perhaps using tents as well as hotels, the actual mileage covered being only incidental. The combination and rider takes a breather after climbing a pass in the Ardennes area of Belgium.

In the days before purpose-designed pannier equipment was manufactured, the only way to carry your camping gear was to lash it on the back of the bike. There were many variations on how this was best achieved. At worst it was simply piled on the back and lashed down with rope, fine if you were good at knots or the trailing ends didn't catch in the chain. There was a lot of ex WD surplus around in the fifties, and these two BSAs parked under the Clifton Suspension bridge in Bristol utilised not just army kit bags, but also a lot of camouflaged tents, sleeping bags and cooking equipment, all secured with webbing. The added weight of all this camping gear tended to upset the bike's steering, a particular hazard made worse when loading after a night's heavy rainfall when everything was soaking wet.

Above left: The alternative to camping was to rent a caravan. Here this Triumph outfit is being used as transport to and from the caravan, thus leaving space for additional passenger room. It is not difficult to understand why people should choose this as an option. The dryness and warmth of a covered-in living space contrasted with the soggy reality of normal British summers. The questionable pleasures of waking up from a night spent in a rain-soaked tent to a showery breakfast cooked on a dodgy Primus Stove, and then having to get on the bike to continue the holiday was somewhat addressed by booking a place at a caravan site.

Above right: Harry Kitts, from Falmouth, took his family and friends on holiday to Weymouth in the summer of 1957. They were riding what was at the time a nearly new Ariel Twin with a matching sidecar. They left it outside the boarding house one night, as they always did, but come the morning they discovered that some ne'er-do-well had stolen the complete magdyno. Since that made the outfit immovable they reported the theft to the Police, but in order to get the bike to run again they had to find an Ariel dealer in the town and buy a whole new Lucas Magdyno, fit it and retime it. They never found out who the thief was, and it took the edge off what had been up to that point a very enjoyable holiday. PHOTO D KITTS

Below: Below: An idyllic summer's day, summer frocks, birds singing, and all's well with the world. You didn't have to wrap up against the elements all the time and this image suggests that the countryside was the best place to be on such a day. The camping stove is on, the water is boiling and the tea leaves are in the pot. The rigid-framed Triumph gleams in the sun, although it's a bit chilly and cardigans are still required, together with a wind shield for the stove.

This has probably got to be the winner in the 'how many on a bike' competition. It shows Doc Kitts at the top of the pile and beneath are fellow members of the Falmouth Territorial Army, Percy Blewett, Lloyd Kitts, Stanley Richards and Gilbert. They were on camp in Alderney, and actually managed to get the little James to run a few feet before they all collapsed in a great giggling pile. Doc was a Cornish nickname for anyone who had an unusual first name; in this case, Renfield Kitts.
PHOTO D KITTS

BSAs 250cc C12 was designed as a bread and butter commuter bike with few pretensions to style or speed. Ray Milton bought his 1957 version with this in mind so that he could make the daily journey from his home at Pilning near Severn Beach, to the Wills' cigarette factory in the centre of Bristol. It is well equipped for the job, having a set off 'Rodark' panniers, leg shields and an after market handlebar-mounted screen. Ray's son, Andrew, sits astride the bike. Pilning was very near to the old Aust Ferry, which before the Severn Bridges were built, was the only way of getting vehicles across the estuary into South Wales without going all the way up to Gloucester.   PHOTO A MILTON

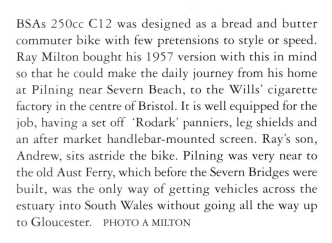

George Gunningham lived in the Bedminster area of Bristol and used his 1957 BSA A10 Road Rocket to get to work, but only during the summer months. For the rest of the year he relied on a little Frances Barnett, he did not want to get his lovely new BSA dirty, or even risk dropping it on the greasy streets. George added his own touches to the BSA; there was the plastic leopard-skin seat cover, the front number plate mounted above the headlight and the useful carrier. He is wearing warm but not very waterproof clothing which included an ex American Air Force fleece jacket; quite cosy but made out of very soft leather and not really designed to protect George's fragile body in the event of a mishap.   PHOTO G GUNNINGHAM

Like most British summers, 1959 provided some sunshine, some clouds and quite a lot of rain. In Weymouth there was a caravan site that hired out small touring caravans, the type with a sloping back designed for an average family of two adults and two kids to live in. That didn't really stop these three motorcyclists, and their three friends from renting one for a week in August. And what a jolly time they had! George is on his 1957 197cc James with his mate Terry on a 225cc James, sitting astride their specially equipped motorcycles whilst friend number three watches from the caravan door; inside and keeping their heads down; the others are in the middle of a game of cards. PHOTO G GUNNINGHAM

Mervyn Pearce on his new 350cc model 16MS AJS arrives early one morning at his place of work in Wadebridge, Cornwall. The year is 1955 and Merv had just part-exchanged his old BSA C11 side-valve for the AJS which was fitted with a screen and leg shields and which aided weather protection immensely. W D Williams was a firm of small builders and undertakers, and Merv was a carpenter whose duties included the making of coffins. The Commer lorry is a flat bed of the 'load it and unload it by hand' variety, whilst the Austin 'three way' was used as a general purpose furniture van.   PHOTO M PEARCE

Originally this Reliant was a milk float in Penryn. Morcom Moyle passed his driving test in it, despite some difficulties in mastering the controls. It had an Austin Seven engine, no synchromesh, and the brakes were very poor. Despite the girder forks, inside the cab it had proper car type controls. Morcom and his father ran a fruit and vegetable business, and they got good service out of this little vehicle, delivering to their customers and getting fish and vegetables from the farms and harbours. Eventually they had to sell it, and it was bought by Ivey Mollard a local car dealer, whose son went on to use it in The Land's End Trial. Morcom remembered seeing it go up Blue Hills with no problems at all; this was due to the low gearing and weight distribution. PHOTO M MOYLE

Right: Morcom Moyle bought this Bond when he was sixteen. Although an avid motorcyclist now, his parents would not let him own a motorcycle at that age, but Morcom swears that the little car was in fact three times more dangerous than any bike that he ever owned. To start it, you had to lift the bonnet and kick start it. Then the pantomime started when you had to try and get back in before the engine stalled. There was no front brake, the lights were like candles and all in all it was pretty grim. Eventually Morcom did manage to swap it for a bike, it was the time of Suez and the Bond had petrol coupons, making it much more desirable than might otherwise have been the case. PHOTO M MOYLE

Below: Jimmy Pack shows off his plunger-framed BSA Golden Flash at Monks Orchard in the mid nineteen fifties. Possibly he had dragged the bike out specifically to get his photo taken, certainly his casual dress including the slippers suggest that on this occasion at least he was not going to take it for a ride up the road. BSAs 650cc parallel twins were very popular and successful machines. They cost £191.10s when new, and were often found attached to sidecars hauling large double-adult versions with complete families inside. Solo there was a fair turn of speed, although the plunger-style rear suspension was improved by the fitting of a more conventional swinging arm just a year or so later. PHOTO HALSGROVE CHS

Amongst many policemen and women there was a great deal of interest in motorcycles which were still very much part of the Bobby-on-the-beat's everyday experience at the time this photo was taken. Most forces issued their rural constables with small motorcycles; BSA C15s were popular, as were the LE Velocette, and in the sixties the Triumph Saint was introduced for high-speed work. At this gathering of early motorcycles a policeman is in deep conversation with one of the organisers about the rigid Triumph. For sure there's not a lot of Mods and Rockers activity to sort out at this meeting!

Above: The business of F H Brackpool had been long established in Forest Hill, South East London and held agencies for many manufacturers. The signs above the window indicate that here you could buy with confidence Douglas, AJS, Panther, BSA, James, Matchless and Ariel motorcycles and spares. If you needed services such as reboring or resleeving then they were the specialists you could go to. On sale outside is a selection of new and used models, from lightweights like the little Corgi scooter (right), through to BSA sidecar outfits. Brackpool's closed down in the late sixties.

Top left: The AA used BSAs, the RAC used Nortons. A generalisation of course, but in this picture taken from an RAC advert the young lady on the Vespa who has broken down is being attended to by a patrolman who is about to work his mechanical magic and get her back on the road pronto. The RAC, from the time that motorcycling was in its infancy, had formed a branch to look after the interests of motorcyclists and to foster the improvement of their machines. From 1920 to 1968 RAC combinations served out on the road, and Watsonians built a special sidecar called the Bambox to go with the ES2 Nortons. The last of the sidecars, operating in the Rhonda Valley, was withdrawn in 1968. PHOTO RAC

Left: The Automobile Association was formed in 1903, initially to combat police persecution and to warn of speed traps. At first all patrols were done on bicycles, but in 1912 motorcycles started to be issued for use by the AA scouts. In 1919 'Road Service Outfits' became a regular sight on the main roads of Britain, and by the late thirties there were 1500 motorcycle patrols and surprisingly still 800 bicycle-mounted operatives. The once familiar AA box, mounted in lay-bys on most major highways was the base for the motorcycle patrols, which were responsible for set routes and stretches of road. By the sixties motorcycles were becoming dated, and mini vans with proper radios eventually took over. This little tin plate coin box shows a BSA M21 with its attendant patrolman as they would have appeared in the late fifties.

Above left: In obscure attics, neglected garages, tumbledown sheds and beneath rotting tarpaulins there remained still in the sixties examples of long-lost makes of motorcycle. The Vintage Motor Cycle Club was formed with the aim of preserving these machines in order that the younger generations might have some idea of the history of motorcycling in this country. Collectors, just a few, would go out and seek such hidden treasures. At the time they were worth very little, no one then appreciated the fact that they might soar in value and cost tens of thousands of pounds to buy today. Here is a Henley, with its Blackburn engine in a pretty much complete state, whilst leaning against it is a Raleigh. The Henley was made in Birmingham in the mid twenties and is quite a rare thing to find these days. The Nottingham-built lightweight Raleigh was a junior member of a family which in the twenties produced machines from a tiny 174cc unit construction side-valves up to very fast 500 ohv's with flat-twins and v-twins in between

Above right: The Wee Mcgregor was an obscure 170cc two-stroke made in Coventry from 1912 to 1924, and was typical of the myriad lightweights being produced at that time. This one has seen better days, and was offered for sale in 1959. Despite being in good condition, it was not a terribly desirable machine. There is a quote from Phil Smith who wrote for the VMCC journal in March 1959 about one such machine that he was offered from King's scrapyard in Coventry. 'I was offered an Indian (too big to run), a Wee McGregor (no self respecting motorcyclist

would be seen on one of these moped-like lightweights) and a single speed Triumph (too old to bother with), all for ten shillings each. No business resulted however for these prices were about normal for the days.

Left: In earlier times there was, at least for the ordinary clubman rider, no distinction between what you rode to work and what you entered in competitions. Here, at a mid fifties hill climb at Trengwainton, near Penzance, John Davey guns his Ariel twin up the hill in an attempt to get fastest time of the day. You had to remove the headlight, just in case you crashed and the glass went on the track, but otherwise the Ariel, with its Anstey link rear fork, is pretty much standard even to the presence of the tax disc near the headlamp shell. The last event took place in 1976 at Trengwainton after which the National Trust took it over.

'Although the Ford is parked outside in the road, it's quite expensive to use everyday to go to work which is only a mile or so up, the road anyway. Still that's a long way to go on a push bike, and, well I thought I would treat myself and get a little moped that would do the journey in half the time, and I wouldn't have to pedal. I can store it round the back; put it in the corridor if necessary so it won't get wet. When I have to go on nights the lights are better than the push bike, and I can actually carry my wife on the back if I can get her to stay on without being afraid of falling off!' NSU made around a million of these little mopeds, and sold them widely across Europe, the ideal commuter bike!

Below: Denis Jenkinson, the rider of this machine, was in later years known as 'The Elder Statesman' of British Racing journalists. Starting work at the Royal Aircraft Establishment at Farnborough during the Second World War, Jenks progressed through two- and four-wheel sporting achievements, including that of being passenger to Eric Oliver when he won the World Sidecar Championship in 1949. His most famous competitive event was when he acted as navigator to Stirling Moss in the 1955 Mille Miglia. He constructed various drag and sprint specials in the sixties, and later became involved with the Brooklands Museum. This fine action shot of Jenks shows his NorBSA, a tuned Gold Star engine in a modified and lowered Norton frame.

Until the nineteen fifties the wearing of pith helmets was seen by most people as necessary for people of European origin to wear in order to avoid sunburn in tropical climes. It was also a badge of the Colonials, both military and civilian. These two, on their lightweight James motorcycle are pictured beneath the blazing African sun doing their duty, dressed in the particular style of the men and women who served in the far-flung outposts of the British Empire. In truth, they were also probably very bored and looking for a bit of excitement which the little motorcycle might provide. The Colonies and Dominions were of course very important markets for British manufacturers; the machines which were exported all over the world earned good revenues for both the companies and the country.

Below: Alan Freke of Bristol on his 1954 Triumph T110 in April 1963. Crudely painted in red by a previous owner, the bike served Alan well until he sold it a few years later to someone who wanted the engine and gearbox for a Douglas Special. The Special was duly sprinted, but eventually the engine blew up, after which the bike was stored in a shed until the nineties. It was rescued by a Douglas enthusiast who provided it with a proper Douglas engine and put it back on the road again. Similarly the Triumph rose from the ashes and has also been re-engined and put back into full working order. It is remarkable that two bikes have been scrapped, one of them twice, and yet they still both exist. It perhaps highlights the green re-cycling credentials of motorcycling. PHOTO ALAN FREKE

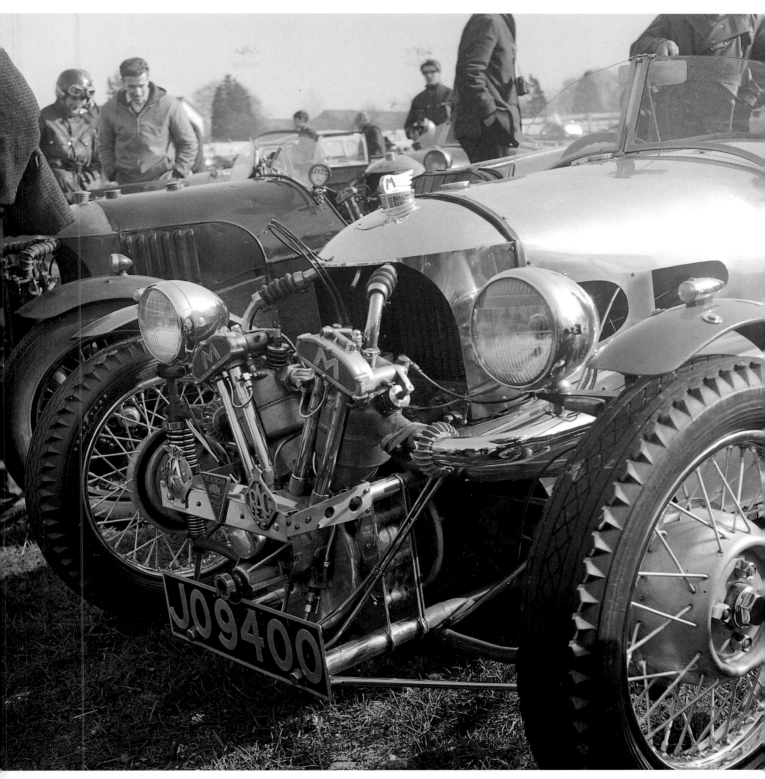

Matchless supplied their V-twin engines to Morgans from 1933 up until the production of three wheelers in this form finished with the outbreak of World War Two. This particular model was photographed at an early Morgan Club meeting, when it was just beginning to be realised that these unique and unconventional machines should be preserved. The Matchless engine had replaced the JAP as the main motive power, and it powered the Super Sports model to give a performance far superior to that of the BSA three-wheeler, the only other similar vehicle available in some quantity during the mid to late thirties.

This picture was taken in 1959 and the background feature, the Aveling & Porter steam roller, would only have a few more years in work before it, like its railway-based cousins, would go out of service for ever. The motorcycles are a pair of Royal Enfield 600cc twins, probably bought from the same dealer as their registration numbers SRL 908 and SRL 651 are very close. It is not easy to see who the road locomotive belongs to, but it is probable that it belonged to Dingles of Stoke Climsland who had a number of such rollers. They were used for the building and maintenance of roads in Devon and Cornwall and, together with the gangs and equipment that went with the job, were a huge presence in the Westcountry in the post war years. It was not uncommon to find a steam roller in a layby on its own at night, gently simmering away, ready for an early start the next morning. Perhaps these two riders stopped to capture a final moment in the history of these wonderful old machines. PHOTO FRAN PARKER

It's half way through the Trial and its time for a tea break. These two eating their sandwiches and drinking tea, bought from the mobile canteen with its Bedford Lorry support vehicle, are warming up after a cold and muddy ride. The sidecar outfit is mostly BSA, but the front down-tube has been made into an oil tank by cutting out the original tubes and replacing them with this enormous bit of pipe. Presumably it must have worked well, although the welding would have to be of high standard to prevent the head stem from coming away from the rest of the bike in steep sections where great forces can act on this area of the frame.

Triumph made another effort at redesigning their range of twins at the end of the fifties, and produced an enclosed version of the 500cc and 350cc models, called respectively the Speedtwin and Twenty One. They were commonly known as the bathtub models because of their shape. Here Peter Old, seated on his 1960 Twenty One is ready for a night out at Pentire in Newquay in the summer of 1967. It shows the kind of efforts a young man about town had to make, not just to look good, but also to try and keep warm and dry for the ride home after an evening at 'The Blue Lagoon'.

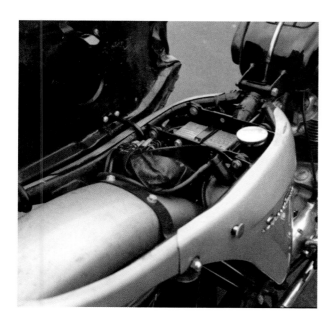

You had to be prepared for breakdowns. From the earliest times manufacturers provided tools to be carried in or on their products. In the beginning it was thought necessary to only provide a bent-wire screwdriver and a couple of combination pressed-steel bicycle spanners. Riders improvised their own gear, and ended up carrying quite large quantities of tools, spares, tow ropes, pumps and inner tubes, just in case. As machines became more reliable there was less need to think about, in terms of unforeseen stoppages, yet the tools were there because motorcyclists used them to do their own maintenance. BSA of course produced a whole range of their own spanners for commercial use; AKD did the same. Triumph provided a very handy tool roll which was secured neatly beneath the dual seat and generally fitted all the nuts and bolts on their bikes, which in this case is a Tiger 110.

Created by John Melzinuk in the late fifties, this double Triumph engined machine was named 'Parasite' (one engine feeding off the other geddit?). It used two T110 engines timed as one, and the gearbox only utilised second and third gears. It was very quick, and was timed at 150 mph at the end of a quarter mile timed run. Eventually it was sold to Don Hyland of New England, who brought it across the Atlantic in the early sixties for a few demonstration runs at airfields in the South of England. It is now back in the US and has been restored by its first owner.

Each year the British motorcycle trade supported shows; the big one was at Earls Court in London, but this publicity photograph was taken in Manchester in the early sixties. It does contrast rather with similar pictures taken during the golden times of the twenties, when almost literally hundreds of makers would be showing off their wares for the general public to drool over. Here are examples of the few remaining manufacturers trying to persuade buyers that their product was the right thing to buy. There is still no evidence in this shot of the Japanese invasion, but it was just a few years away. Notice too the presence of bicycle manufacturers; sometimes, like Vindec and Sunbeam, they too had made powered two-wheelers in the distant past.

Petrol was 5/6d a gallon, and you could buy an Austin A30 for £175. From the showroom you could purchase a new Lambretta or BMW, and there were some ex police Triumph Saints on offer as well. The garage also held a Honda agency, and although there were still only smaller bikes for sale (after all it was commonly agreed at the time that the Japanese could not make big bikes) the writing was on the wall. Perhaps the story here is that someone had got fed up with the Vincent and had decided to trade it in for a smaller and more easily handled Honda Black Bomber. Whatever, the dealer seems to appreciate the qualities of his big v-twin, and may possibly just hang on to it for a while, just for old times sake! In fact Ross Motors of Hinkley in Leicestershire specialised in Vincents and bought and sold them long after they had gone out of production. The 1956 series D has a side oil tank, a buddy seat and a girdraulic fork.

Below: A scene so typical of British industry and home workshops throughout the land. The Bush radio in the window is on full blast, the lathe beats out its merry hum, intermingled with an occasional strangled whine when the oil runs out or too much pressure is used. Swarf builds up and drops on the floor making boots with thick soles something of a must. An old hand drill and set of callipers hang on the wall. This is the kind of machine that produced some of the finest motorcycles the world ever saw, and the person working it shows immense engineering skills and craftsmanship. Old fashioned lathes such as this one are no longer built in this country, far eastern computer aided devices have almost entirely replaced such out of date technologies.

Crash Helmets were not made compulsory wear until 1973, and if you were an old-time motorcyclist you tended to scoff at any form of head protection other than a flat hat or beret. Many claimed that because there was much reduced hearing and vision, crash helmets in fact impeded safety. This shot of a rider in Bridport illustrates the uniform of many people at the time. Barbour jacket and trousers, stiff leather boots, and flat hat with goggles. Often there was a compulsory cigarette on the go to aid concentration. The bike is a Dot Trials THX with either a 197 or 246cc engine. Dots were made in Manchester and were powered by Villiers engines, their trademark Earles-type leading links with short arms and long hydraulically damped units being very noticeable in this shot.

Opposite: The rider of this BSA Bantam in a Trial is wearing the classic thorn-proof Barbour suit, together with a 'corker' helmet. In 1963 the wearing of helmets was being discussed in the press; a letter writer of the time suggested that he was against its use in Trials because of the low speeds involved, heat fatigue, loss of individuality with regard to photographs, it was unlikely to set an example to the general public and the fact that compulsion was not attractive to anybody. The case for wearing head protection put forward by another correspondent was that of riders' safety and to give a more attractive public image. Mr Marples, the Minister of Transport at the time, would end up making the wearing of helmets a legal requirement for all motorcyclists on public roads, so you may as well wear it anyway.

A group of young people at Brands Hatch in the early sixties. Clearly they are all motorcyclists, but they also show their affiliation to a specific subgroup; they are Rockers. This phenomenon grew out of the Teddy Boy era and was soon to become infamous as the other half of the Mods versus Rockers battles which so delighted the Sunday newspapers. The Rockers rode big, British bikes and liked doing ton-up riding; they listened to rock & roll music and regarded Mods as weedy and effeminate. Here at Brands however, at least some of them have arrived in an old Ford Zephyr, and they are dressed to impress the female members of the group.

By contrast to the group of Rockers at Brands Hatch, this photograph of a young man at Weston Super Mare and riding a Bristol registered Matchless G11 650 Twin was taken in the same year. He is wearing a jumper, sensible shoes and grey flannels. The bike is not modified in any way except to have a set of Craven panniers, specifically designed for touring, on the back of his machine. It is a far cry from the fashion statements being made by the Rockers, yet it still conveys the impression of a dedicated rider with a well prepared bike who is enjoying his time at the seaside.

If ever there was a rider that you might want to come across in the sixties, it would be Mike Hailwood. He is seen here just before the start of the 1963 Junior TT in the Isle of Man, and the bike is a 350cc MV. Experts suggested that the race would be between Hailwood, Jim Redman on a Honda Four and John Hartle on the Italian Gilera. The MV, which was slower and heavier than the Honda, was having handling problems. Hailwood was riding near his limit and the bike was snaking badly through Sulby before he was forced to retire with the MV firing on only two cylinders. Redman went on to win with Hartle second. Hailwood, along with his young daughter, was killed in a tragic road accident in 1981 at the age of 40.

Below: On a hot day its worth pausing in the main street of Ottery to finish your ice cream or lollipop, and fantasise about the bike you would really like. All the young bloods are experts of course and can quote figures, The 1955 BSA B31 was good for 70mph and could churn out 17bhp from its 348cc engine. It was based around the M series bottom half, and had a bigger 500cc brother called the B33. It was not a Gold Star, although there were quite a few common parts, and you could do one up to look like a Goldie if you wanted. No one was fooled by the iron engine and pedestrian looks of course. Meanwhile, 'The Great Escape' with the famous Steve McQueen jump was playing again at the pictures, so there is no time to hang about discussing such matters if you want to see the film for the third time. PHOTO HALSGROVE CHS

It's surprising how different racing sidecars are to normal everyday bolt-on jobs. For a start it would be difficult to ride the bike as a solo if the chair was taken off. Passenger comfort was the last thing to worry about, as long as there were enough hand holds! The passenger also needed complete faith in his driver, the agility of a trapeze artist and an intimate knowledge of the circuit. There were few takers for this less-than-glamorous job, even though the crewman worked at least as hard as the driver. This is quite a rare Royal Enfield engined outfit, the frame has been stretched and lowered to accommodate the motor, and the fibre glass shell fits neatly around the whole ensemble.

This Reliant Regal three-wheeler car was technically a motorcycle and sidecar; at least that was what it was as far as the licensing authorities were concerned. You could tax it as a sidecar, and it could be driven on a motorcycle licence. Despite its later reincarnation as Del Boys main means of transport, for many years it provided a bridge between two-wheeled vehicles and the all-pervasive car. Motorcyclists with families could use them and still maintain that they had not given up the freedom of their favoured form of transport. In truth however they were always looked down on by both car owners and motorcyclists. Nevertheless they had a strong following, and Regals were produced in various guises from 1953 to 1973. They had a bit of reputation for tipping over. Mr Bean exploited this to comic effect, however driven properly they were no more difficult or dangerous to drive than any other kind of vehicle.

Yes it was this easy to pick up, no there was no reverse, yes it was tiny. The Peel dates from the time of Dr Beeching's rail closures in the early sixties and was made in the Isle of Man from 1962 to 1965. It had a 49cc DKW engine and was fully roadworthy. It is celebrated as the smallest production road legal car ever to have been made. It was very light and could be picked up and pushed like a trolley; the manufacturer's provided a small drawer-like handle for that very purpose at the back. Jeremy Clarkson, on 'Top Gear', drove one through Central London, and then proceeded to drive into the BBC studios, along the corridors and into his office, thereby demonstrating that it was a viable machine, although possibly not the most practical.

At 1732 feet above sea level, Tan Hill Pub in North Yorkshire is reckoned to be the highest inn in England. The BSA M20 pictured here looks to be the kind that the AA used for their patrols, although of course the sidecar would have been changed. With the engine enclosed in its little fairing the engine could get very hot. It is said that under certain conditions the BSA M20 engine would glow red hot, an alarming although ultimately not dangerous state of affairs; even so when this phenomenon was seen at night it could be just a little off putting.

This couple on their Vespa scooter seem to epitomise the height of respectability. Their very English style of clothing contrasts somewhat with what the Mods might be wearing on their forays down to Brighton a few years later. It is of course exactly what the designers had in mind when they produced the scooter, with its all-enclosed engine and flat floorboards it was supposed to be clean and easily maintained. No oil streaks or petrol stains for these two! The little open wicker shopping basket on the front and the spare wheel in case of a puncture on the rear carrier were all part of the package. Vespa is Italian for Wasp, and the Piaggio Company which produced these bikes in the early fifties had amongst its customer such luminaries as John Wayne, Audrey Hepburn and Gregory Peck.

Vespa's great rival, the Lambretta, started scooter production a year after Vespa in 1947. The name was derived from the River Lambro which ran next to the factory in Milan. This mid fifties shot, probably of an Li 150 model, although details are obscured by the clothing, again shows the kind of buying public which the manufacturer's sought. Beside one of the newly-opened dual carriageways, in a rest stop or 'layby' as it came to be known, the two girls have stopped for a bite to eat. The sun shines and the traffic thunders past, but the summer outing is not to be spoiled. Note the big handlebar screen  designed to keep not just the wind and rain away from the riders, but useful to deflect flies and other flying obstacles that tend to make a mess on clean clothes.

Scooter time! This pair of Lambrettas, one a TV 175 series 2, and the other a LI 150 series 1 are pictured flanking a late forties Ford Anglia in Llangain, Camarthenshire. The photograph itself was taken some years after the car, and indeed the scooters were originally made. They were probably being used as first vehicles on which to learn to drive and hopefully to pass driving tests. Certainly the looks of the car would have dated by the mid sixties but it has been customised with after market port holes for the bonnet, white wall tyres and grill badges with spotlights. However the shape and style of the scooters meant that their credibility with the younger generation outlasted that of their four-wheeled stable mate. This would have been around the time that Mods were emerging as a fashion, although this group may not have all been pin ball wizards. PHOTO HALSGROVE CHS

The quiet country roads of North Yorkshire meander between drystone walls and isolated farms. A sunny afternoon is a good time for an outing on the scooters, but there is also a bubble car attached to the group. The Messerschmitt was manufactured by the German aircraft firm after the Second World War, at a time when they were forbidden to make aircraft. The little 191cc Sachs-engined three wheeler used a tandem seating arrangement, the passenger sat directly behind the driver thus making the vehicle more stable. There was no steering wheel as such, rather a sort of handlebar beneath the canopy, and a switch to make the engine run backwards in order to provide a reverse gear. They could get up to 55mph, and would have been capable of giving the scooters a run for their money.

Norway is not a place normally associated with motorcycle or scooter production, nevertheless the firm of Tempo made an attempt to introduce into this country a range of their products in the early sixties. By entering some of their machines in competitions, they hoped to generate publicity that would help sales. Here is a Progress scooter powered by a 192cc Sachs motor being ridden along a rough track, trying to prove itself. It had eighteen-inch wheels, a dynastart and weighed 160 kilos. In fact the Progress was too heavy and too late to catch the scooter boom, and only a few were ever sold in the UK. Not the most practical machine.

One of the largest dealers in the London area was Comerfords of Thames Ditton in Surrey. They held the main agencies for many of the leading British and Foreign companies, and they were very strong supporters of the competition side of the industry. Pre war they had been involved in marketing a speedway bike called the Comerford Wallis, but after the war they decided to sponsor many riders using their own or factory-prepared bikes. Comerfords not only sold a vast range of bikes, they had warehouses full of second hand trade-ins, but they also sold cars, three wheelers and combinations. An eclectic mix of bikes was always on offer here; in the photograph there can be identified Triumph, Greeves, Husqvarna, Velocette, BSA and of course the beautiful rigid framed pre war Triumph which is in the forefront of the picture.

One way of proclaiming to the world that both your bike and your good taste were superior to the rest of the herd was by putting extra lights on your pride and joy. This Triumph Tiger 110 has a total of twelve lights and two horns, and they all appear to be wired up. The power output of the poor Triumph's generator must have been fully stretched to cope with that lot, especially if most were on at the same time. Still, the onlookers seem impressed, and it's doubtful if you could find a more polished specimen for many miles around. The indicators, although universal now, were something of an innovation at the time although the crash bars, badge bar and fairing were all extras that could be purchased over the counter to suit your particular bike.

Right: At the shows the people on the stand always have to deal with an excited, often knowledgeable group of young children, all demanding facts, figures, leaflets and a sit on the bike. Of course this has to be tolerated, and encouraged, they are after all the next generation of buyers and cannot be disillusioned at such an early stage of their lives. This photo of a Triumph Saint could be the one which Neale Shilton, who was the hard-riding General Sales Manager at the factory, rode to one of the German Shows right in the heart of BMW country where he was trying to get government orders. Exports were very important, and this bike was specially designed for police work, carrying a wireless and various other bits of equipment that could be used to help with law enforcement.

Opposite, top: The admiring crowd gather around as the little James 'Grand Prix' sidecar outfit is pushed into life. The sidecar passenger hangs on, perhaps wishing that he had stuck to his tricycle, big brother opens the throttle and dad grunts with the effort of getting the whole lot moving. These specials were often constructed with the idea of 'bringing the kids on'. For some this worked well, others who perhaps were not quite so adept at learning how to control the plot might be put off for life. The sight of a terrified youngster grimly hanging on to a bike headed out of control toward a bramble bush, whilst its rider cannot remember that by simply closing the throttle he could slow the bike down, was not an uncommon sight. Gran in the background keeps her thoughts to herself, and has another puff of her fag.

Opposite, bottom: These two armed guards are looking after one of the most iconic machines of the fifties and sixties This BSA Gold Star is a big fin DBD34 and its all kitted out with the modified bits and pieces which were available from suppliers such as Eddie Dow. The specially developed fibre glass tank, the racing seat, the clip on handlebars and rear sets are all evident. The swept back exhaust and silencer produced a unique twittering sound on the overrun, whilst the bark of the big single was all part of the package. In this sort of state the bike looked as though it was a racer, indeed its successful competition history was what made it sell long after its performance was equalled and exceeded by its bigger 650cc twin-cylinder brother. They were notoriously difficult to start, the clutch had to be gradually let out otherwise it would stall, and the riding position was very uncomfortable. But few other machines gained the kind of respect that the Goldie had.

Below: Poor little thing, it really wasn't designed for this! Frances Barnett made a variety of lightweight two strokes, basic commuter machines that were cheap and simple to maintain. They all had Villiers engines, and were mostly named after birds; Falcon, Kestrel, Plover, Merlin, Snipe. The scene is Station Road in Princetown, close to Dartmoor Prison. It's the early 1960s and there were still vestiges of the railway, which had closed down in 1956, to be seen. The winter of 1963 was just a year away; the big freeze would cut off many parts of Dartmoor for months. Enjoying the summer sun were Louis Brown, Olive Brown and Maureen Ellis, unaware of the many months of Arctic weather that was just around the corner. PHOTO HALSGROVE CHS

Opposite, top: The ghostly image of a vintage motorcycle emerges from the bushes and passes on its way, but the parked spectators' bikes provide much interest. The spectrum is wide, the little Raleigh Runabout with the 'L' plates belonged to an enthusiastic but poverty-stricken student, whilst the Lambretta scooter was owned by his older brother who was able to afford something with a little more credibility. The Norton leaning against the tree is a different thing altogether, it being a virtual Manx Norton racer out on road plates, with no lights and a standard exhaust system instead of the usual megaphone. The 'Inters' were only built to special order from the mid fifties, the BSA Gold Star proving too great a rival for Norton to catch in terms of sales.

Opposite, bottom: This 1911 Triumph was bought new by the grandfather of the man standing beside it. The place is Tregear Farm near St Ewe in Cornwall, and the bike is a single speed roadster. The setting is very rural, the roads are narrow and the valleys steep. In order to start the bike you have to pedal furiously, and planning a route is essential. It is not easy to pedal away uphill, and if failure occurs, as it can so easily, then there is little alternative but to go back and either have another go at the hill, or choose a different way round. The farmer standing here said that he could just about recall bikes being in the barns before the war, but they disappeared soon after that, presumably, apart from this survivor, the rest went to make Spitfires

Below: It is not an unusual place to stop on an early VMCC Club outing; pubs seem to be one of the natural homes of motorcyclists. Ixion wrote at length on the subject of Inns, they had played a substantial role in his young motorcycling career and he discovered that from the date of buying his first motorcycle he had spent far more time and money at these places than he had reckoned on. It was not so much the drink, as the warmth, comfort and hospitality that pubs offered and the fact that they often played hosts to the start and finish of events, they had rooms available for meetings and could lay on a good spread at 'Do's'. They were really the club, he reckoned! In the picture can be seen three Triumphs, an Indian and two Douglases; all waiting for the riders to stop talking, finish their drink and just get on with it.

Round the back of most dealers was a place where traded in machines were stored. It was a place, depending on your personal inclination, where hidden gems could be discovered, cheap hacks could be bought or spare parts sourced. Here can be seen the products of BSA, NSU, Raleigh, Lambretta, Ariel, Austin and various bicycle manufacturers such as Vindec and Humphries & Dawes. The smart looking BSA Bantam Trials machine has many innovative parts, and should have been a very competitive ride for its creator.

This tattered photograph of a unit construction 247cc New Imperial came with the bike from its St Blazey shed where it had lain for forty years and pretty much reflects the condition of the poor little bike when found. It had the registration number ANE, and was affectionately known as 'Annie'. New in 1933, it had survived the war years then been traded in for a new Ariel. No one really wanted it, and it lay in a shed where gradually rain had eaten through the corrugated iron roof and dripped steadily onto the tank. Now it had been rescued and the damage assessed. The tank had a hole in the top, and an even bigger hole in the bottom. The water had eroded the alloy chaincases and one of the bottom rails was just about corroded through. Job for someone else! A collector of the marque bought it for spares.

Below: This well-worn postcard was sent in 1904, and depicts a competitor on the very wet Pioneer Run of that year. 'All good wishes from Cecil and Lucy Usher' it says. It shows just how vulnerable the passengers on early forecars were. In any small incident the person sitting, unsecured, in the front could be thrown or otherwise unceremoniously dumped from their perch. They took the brunt of the weather, and in this wonderful shot, the umbrella is proving extremely useful in keeping off most of the rain. The driver, seated high above his sheltering partner is obliged to take extra care to make sure nothing untoward might occur on his 1904 machine.

Velocette motorcycles were a firm from Hall Green in Birmingham who produced a range of very successful single-cylinder motorcycles. This picture shows a Venom which was prepared for the long and arduous 500 mile race at Thruxton airfield in 1960. It was entered by Shipton-on-Stour Velocette agent Arthur Taylor, and ridden by Rex Avery and Ken Douglas. It came a very creditable sixth place, not bad for a road registered machine. Development work on Velocettes like this led to the creation of their last and probably most sought after machines, named after this race – the Thruxton.

In February 1971 the firm of Velocette finally closed its doors and production of one of the best loved British motorcycles finally came to an end. Velocette chose to cease manufacture in the face of the Japanese onslaught, the old-fashioned single-cylinder four strokes being no longer wanted except by a few enthusiasts. The factory was boarded up, the gates locked, and the offices cleared. In the car park, blowing in the wind having escaped the bonfire in the barrel, were unwanted brochures for the flat twins, the Vogue and the LE. Amongst the debris was this business card, a survivor with burn marks, from Hall Green.

'The BSA', as it was known locally, is seen here in the final years of the Small Heath factory's existence. Having been the centre of one of the largest motorcycle manufacturing empires in the world, within a few short weeks of this photo being taken the factory would finally and irretrievably close down, and Armoury Road would become another distant memory. At this stage the factory was only making components and fittings, production having been transferred to Meriden. Golden Hillock Road, along which the cars are travelling, crossed over a canal and railway at this point, all at one time used to service the factory which had been opened originally in 1862.

Below: Another of the specials that was created was this Norjap. It consisted of a roadgoing Norton Atlas frame, into which someone had shoehorned a 750cc JAP (that is J A Prestwich), engine. Instead of sourcing a large ohv engine from a rip-roaring Morgan, the builder instead chose one which had originally powered an industrial work truck. The bike looked spectacular, there was no room to spit through it (as an old adage which suggested that this was some form of perfection put it), and handled just like a Norton should. Unfortunately, and even by wringing its neck, it would not go over 55 mph. It also absolutely refused to go when there was the slightest hint of dampness about, the exposed forward facing magneto bearing the full brunt of water from the road and front mudguard.

The grafting of a Triumph engine into a Norton frame produced what was supposed to be the best of both worlds. Superb handling from the featherbed Norton frame, combined with the speed and reliability of Triumph's big 650 engine, it allowed the owner to incorporate his own ideas into the machine, and accessory manufacturers were quite happy to supply those riders who had the money with any amount of bolt-on goodies. Thus this machine has a fibre glass tank, clip on handlebars, alloy guards, rear sets and a large central speedometer. The lights have been removed, and although it is road registered, there is little doubt that it has seen action on the track. The rider's ex War Department coat does not do much for the image or the streamlining of this particular special.

The chopper movement started in the USA when servicemen returning from the Second World War found it difficult to settle down. Some took to the road on motorcycles, and in the film 'The Wild Ones' Marlon Brando depicted this scenario when he is seen leading a bunch of outlaws who are riding British and American machines which have been altered to suit the taste of their riders. This was the beginning of the customising, bobber and chopper story, a whole industry and lifestyle having subsequently developed around this type of bike. This shiny example is a Tri Bsa, consisting of a modified BSA frame with extended forks whilst using a Triumph pre unit engine to create something which is unique and pleasing to the constructor. Interestingly, racers have used the same combination of frame and engine to produce a machine which is totally different from the one in this picture. PHOTO SALLY MADGWICK

Below: Despite what some might perceive as the unfortunate anti social image of motorcycles in the sixties, there have always been enthusiasts who banded together into clubs. In this case it's a family-oriented group of people who prefer to use their motorcycle and sidecars as their everyday means of transport. The machines identifiable in this shot are a Norton with a Watsonian chair together with a BMW and Steib. There is nothing to say where the exact location of this shot is, but the summer clothes, the children's towels and plastic spades together with the sunshine would perhaps suggest a visit to a beach, and judging by the car park, probably on a bank holiday.

The serious faces and rather formal pose of this group of riders suggests that this club may well be in for a cold and wet ride. The bikes are mostly big twins of the early sixties, all kitted out with weather protection and fairings. The sidecars also provide a sometimes less than leakproof covering for the passengers. Weather protection on motorcycles was being seriously addressed at this time, with great efforts by motorcycle and accessory manufacturers going into the design of fibre glass handlebar-mounted half fairings and the all enclosing full fairings, examples of which can be seen here.

Below: The solid good looks of a mid sixties Triumph Thunderbird are captured in this colourful painting. The artist is unknown, but it is signed AJC 1986. Many owners liked to have their bikes immortalised by artists, and there was, and is, a not inconsiderable trade for those who are good with a paintbrush and can get the technical details right. The bike has what appears to be a reallocated number, so it may have been a newly rebuilt model out for the first time.

The old engine house at Condurrow near Redruth, Cornwall, forms the backdrop to this picture of a mid thirties Sunbeam on to which someone seems to have grafted a BSA dual seat. Jim Jennings had his workshop in the Count House of this mine, and always had a stack of interesting motorcycles, principally Vincents. He had in his youth worked for a Vincent dealership in North London and had known the factory and its personnel quite well. When he moved to Cornwall he brought his knowledge and expertise along with him, and became a familiar part of the local scenery. He loved to tell the story about his meeting with Lawrence of Arabia, and how he had once repaired a tyre for him up near Catterick in Yorkshire where Lawrence was based at the time.   PHOTO J JENNINGS

Claire Gunningham tries out a little 98cc James for size in her Dad's front garden at their home in Pill near Bristol. The James had two speeds, operated by a lever on the handlebars. It was not a fast machine, and the revs had to be carefully matched to the road speed before any attempt was made to change gear, a loss of speed or even a stall might result if this was not perfected. Behind Claire is her Dad's Norton with quite a rare VP sidecar, made by the Variable Pitch Company of Cheltenham, a firm who specialised in making aircraft propellers.
PHOTO G GUNNINGHAM

'They were knocking a shed down just round the back, and the bloke who owned it asked me if I wanted the old bikes in there. I can't turn down an offer like that, so I gave him some money and these are what I came away with. One's a 1955 Sun and the other is a 1954 Ambassador. They both have Villiers 197cc 8E engines; they both have three speed gearboxes, although four speeds were an option. I think I sold the Sun to finance the restoration of the Ambassador. I still have it down the shed, but it's not been out for a while, even though I did get it sort of running.'   PHOTO G GUNNINGHAM

St Andrews Road, Par, Cornwall is the setting of this 1927 photograph of P G Rose's Garage. The business was started in the twenties by Mr Rose, seen standing by the right-hand petrol pump. He specialised in cylinder boring, crankshaft regrinding and so on, and he also held a Douglas and AJS dealership. Just before the Second World War, Mr Rose expanded to take on an Opel agency, but German cars were not very popular at the time and he didn't shift many. Mr Rose lost his son at sea during the war, leaving him a broken man, and he eventually sold the business. Most of the motorcycles seen here are AJS machines, with a Douglas and an Enfield making up the numbers.

Below: In 1988 a group of Vintage Motor Cycle Club members came together to re enact the historic photograph. The original building still existed at that time, and unbelievably one of the original AJS bikes, the one on the far left, belonged to a member living just a mile up the road. So, Frank Hawke, Hugh Bicknell, Jack Bacon, Lloyd Watson, Martin Curl, Roger Fogg (the author) and Keith Pearce all lined up for the picture. Hugh Bicknell was on his little two-stroke Enfield, Keith Pearce, the then owner of the garage borrowed Jack Bacons 2¾hp Douglas and all the rest were on AJSs of the correct period. Martin Curl took the photograph on a time lapse camera, which explains how he was able to run forward and leap on to his machine before the shutter clicked. The building has now been demolished to make way for a modern car showroom. PHOTO M CURL

No matter what new technologies the Japanese introduced with their motorcycles, there was nothing they could do to stop the rain. This 1967 publicity shot from Carney Penrice Ltd of Birmingham shows their 'Commuter Suit', a 12oz coverall giving complete neck-to-toe protection, including shoe covering. It was in midnight blue, made of bri-nylon and could be packed away into a small bag if not needed. It was washable, drip dry and sold for £6-19s-6d. There were many other such suits using new materials to replace the more traditional thorn-proof or rubberised-cloth rain suits which were coming on to the market in the sixties. The problem with this is its ok if your clothes are dry to begin with, but if you have wet shoes or trousers and try to get into the suit then there are many strange lumps and bumps which become visible beneath the smooth lines of the suit where trousers have ridden up around the knees and shirts are rolled around elbows.

British actress and model Karen Young poses at Umberslade Hall, BSA's research and development establishment, on a Triumph Bandit. This Works' photograph shows the 349cc overhead camshaft Bandit, which essentially was the same as the BSA Fury, and produced 34bhp making it capable of 117 mph. It was BSA/Triumph's final attempt to take on the Japanese, and prototypes were ready to be tested by the summer of 1972. They had a good reception by the press who were impressed by their handling, oiltight engines and style. An American magazine reckoned that Triumph would sell all they could make in the USA; however it was not to be. BSA found themselves with an £8 million trading loss, and were later forced into partnership with Norton, carrying £20m of debts. Only five Triumph and 8 BSA prototypes remain, nearly all in museums.
PHOTO J VICKERS

Below: 'Historic Route 66', the Mother Road that stretches as the song says 'from Chicago to LA'. North America was an important market for British manufacturers, and their products were held in high esteem in the sixties. This Norton 850cc Commando in Springfield Missouri had a kickstart and was a crowd puller. It had ended up in a small town in the Ozarks, and was owned by a fellow who repaired tractors for a living. It was all OK he said, but the tank was rusting badly from the inside, and flakes continually blocked the fuel lines and caused petrol starvation. This was cured by pouring in tank sealant, after which it would knock spots off a Harley Sportster. Its still there, living with a Mountain Man down near the Arkansas border.

BIBLIOGRAPHY

Motor Cycle Cavalcade, Ixion, 1950, Iliffe

Veteran and Vintage Motor Cycles, James Sheldon, 1961, Batsford

History and Development of Motorcycles, C F Caunter, 1955, HMSO

Motorcycle Parade, Bob Holliday, 1974, David and Charles

Lost Motorcycles of the 1920s, Jack Bacon, 1988, Panther

Britain's Racing Motorcycles, L R Higgins, 1952, Foulis

History of the World's Motorcycles, R Hough and L J K Setright, 1966, George Allen and Unwin

The Veterans, Aldermans Press, 1983

Historical Foreign Motorcycle Scrapbook, 1955, Floyd Clymer

Telling the Tale, R Fogg, Packet Publishing

Century of Motorcycling in Cornwall, R Fogg, 2004, Blue Hills

Motorcycling in the 1930s, Bob Currie, 1981, Hamlyn

British Motorcycles of the '30s, Roy Bacon, 1996, Osprey

Encyclopedia of Motorcycles, Erwin Tragatsch, 2000, Quantum Books

Early Motorcycles, Victor Page, 1971, Post Motor Books

The Sidecar, A History, Geoff Brazendale, 1999

Our Sidecars, Jo Axon, 1988

The Land Beyond the Ridge, Roy K Battson, 1974, Goose & Son

Vintage Road Test Journals 1-6, Titch Allen, 1976, Bruce Main Smith Publications